This book is for you if...

...you are a heart-centred entrepreneur, a therapist, coach, trainer, consultant, alternative practitioner or healer and want to use your natural talents to the best of your abilities through the success of your business – this book is a must-read.

You will discover:
- The seven business angels you need to meet on your sacred soul path.
- A seven-step business angel plan taking you through each business building stage.
- Energy ... it's the life force of all living things and never more so than in our evolutionary age.
- The entrepreneur's biggest dilemma and how to rise above it.
- Discover the significance of business chakras to identify where your business problems are manifesting from.
- Dispel the myths and truths behind your money issues ... and why lack of money isn't your biggest hurdle.
- Discover the quirky workings of your brain ... and why it isn't set to make you successful.
- How to find your magical destiny path ... and escape the labyrinth in the veil of illusion.
- Embrace evolutionary change ... and learn the importance of adding your contribution to the universal database.
- Create the space where miracles happen ... and release your creative genius.
- Intuition, it's your built-in navigation system that never fails.
- How to evolve and take your place in the world – your calling and time is now!

What people are saying about this book

"In this transformational business book, Wendy shows heart-centred business owners how to transform their business by embracing the mystical, scientific, and spiritual aspects that create and underpin the world of business today.

A wonderful resource and treasure trove of inspiration, ideas, and action steps for heart-centred business owners worldwide. She truly is one of life's Business Angels! Wendy effortlessly weaves together the mystical, scientific, and spiritual aspects to life and business, enabling you to take action and transform your business, an incredible gift for sharing the mystical and spiritual aspects of life".

Kimberley Lovell - Spiritual Intuitive Theta Healer & Holistic Business Mentor.

"If you are a heart-centred entrepreneur who has not yet been successful with your business, this book is definitely for you"

"Wendy outlines the business struggles, myths, and cures - what it takes to make your business successful even in these difficult times. It all begins with you and your business both being authentically you. The paradox is that those with the biggest hearts nurture a need to help and heal others on a deep soul level. It is a calling. In doing so, they often forego the need to nurture their business from soul level.

Wendy then sets out a clear path that we can follow through the book to caring for your business mentally, emotionally and spiritually so you both prosper.

Let Wendy guide you through the steps to get you on your journey to success. This book is bang-on".

                                    Norma Reid   www.fromdreamstoreality.ca

"What business school does not tell you. *The 7 Business Angels You Need To Meet* provides a unique insight into how and why your business may not be behaving as expected. Even succeeding beyond your dreams may not be as expected.

Drawing from sources of ancient and modern knowledge, *The 7 Business Angels You Need To Meet* brings clarity and understanding to how we create our business reality.

Sprinkled with emotional anecdotes, the structured journey will create new insights and realisations.

From there, you can see all business and personal situations differently and start to achieve the results you desire.

                                                        Jim J. Doyle,
Business healer, communications coach, keynote speaker.

My name is Wendy Howard, and the reason I wrote *The 7 Business Angels You Need To Meet* is that I discovered building a heart-centred entrepreneurial business is very different to many of the traditional business models. You need a completely different skill set; and you begin a completely different, often deeply mental, emotional, and spiritual personal and business journey to anything you've ever experienced before, or will do so again.

It was through my work and my own business journey that I began to notice patterns in the way people approached their business and the types of similar problems they had, such as difficulties in:

- Attracting the right kind of clients - those willing to invest financially in their services.
- Asking for (and receiving) money in return for their valuable services, or simply giving away their crown jewels receiving little or nothing back in return.
- Seeking out the right help and support to get to the next level of business growth.

- Feeling disillusioned or frustrated after working hard and investing heavily to gain qualifications but client's not recognising the value in this.
- Worthiness and personal value and how to get that message across in a way that resonates with and attracts prospective clients.

Most significantly, I noticed that as an entrepreneur, your business is a direct reflection of what is already going on inside of you. If something isn't right in your inner world in the way you think and feel, in turn your choice of actions will manifest as problems in your business and outer world.

I set out to discover why some heart-centred entrepreneurs are incredibly successful in their businesses - while others continue to struggle or fail regardless of the business lessons they are given or the number of qualifications they achieve.

Was there a switch to success? If so, how can it be turned on?

As part of my research I had the great privilege of interviewing Dr Lisa Turner of Psycademy, and was introduced to the business chakra model. Lisa has spent over twenty years researching and developing this model with amazing results.

Lisa explained that it works like this. In the physical body your energy centre is made up of energy chakras. Chakra means wheel of light.

There are seven in total that govern psychological properties – higher chakras are the mental side, and lower chakras are the instinctive side.

You have chakras, and so does your business as a direct reflection of what is already going on inside of you. Therefore if any of your personal chakras are weak, this will manifest as problems, difficulties, or blocks in your business. In this book I will take you through the business chakra model as explained by Dr Lisa Turner so that you can identify where your chakras are weak, and therefore manifesting as problems in the related area of your business.

I then go further, by giving you seven key steps to your business by identifying the seven business angel profiles related to each business chakra and how by seeking out these individuals, they will support and help you to grow your heart-centred business following a unique Business Angel Plan.

Having gained an initial understanding of the seven key steps to growing your business and relevance to meeting special experts – your business angels to help you at each step, I then take you through a deeper insight into evolution, and the importance of your contribution in the digital communications age. You will learn about the quirky workings of your brain, escape from the veil of illusion and the one degree shift that will change your destiny.

In writing *The 7 Business Angels You Need To Meet* I want to express my deepest gratitude for the generosity of knowledge and information sharing of my many supporters who have helped to bring this book to life - you truly are my business angels!

About the Author

Wendy Howard is often called the 'Business Visionary' for her ability to intuitively see the potential and get to the root cause of where and why problems are manifesting in your business – and give you creative solutions to move forward positively.

Her work is based on the principle that your business is a direct reflection of what is already inside of you, your thoughts, your emotions, and your beliefs. If your business blueprint is congruent with who you are at soul level you will naturally attract the right people and circumstances.

Wendy suggests that with the help of seven business angel mentors, you will discover the business lessons to growing a successful heart-centred business, while at the same time strengthening your personal chakras for increased wealth, health, and happiness in both business and your life.

Wendy has a Masters Degree in Business Management (Cambridge), specialising in Creative & Transformational Change. She is also a qualified Social Care Manager, an earlier career before launching her business Spirit of Venus as an Accelerated Learning Trainer, Business Coach, Theta Healer and Visionary.

Wendy is able to combine research, knowledge, experience, business acumen, creativity, and intuition in a unique way to bring you her first book, *The 7 Business Angels You Need To Meet* a must-have for anyone who is serious about growing a successful heart-centred business.

A Gift for you!

To help you on your business journey along the path of the heart-centred entrepreneur, I've created this website with additional resources you can download and use as part of your personal and business growth.

Visit www.7businessangels.com and enter access code: BAGifts for your downloads.

Business Angel Plan Template

Download a your PDF 7-step Business Angel Plan template to guide you through each business-building step.

Business Angel Wisdom & Insight e-book

Download a collection of valuable wisdom, insights, tips and inspirational quotes from successful business angels across the world. See who you resonate with and how to gain access to them.

Business Destiny Reading

Plus … Information on how to book a unique Business Destiny Reading to help you find direction and release your creative genius. You will receive an audio of your reading and a unique seven-step Business Angel Plan for guidance and setting out your next steps. Details online at www.7businessangels.com

The 7 Business Angels You Need To Meet

The Sacred Path Of Successful Heart-centred Entrepreneurs

By
Wendy Howard

Published by
Filament Publishing Ltd
16, Croydon Road, Waddon, Croydon,
Surrey, CR0 4PA, United Kingdom
Telephone +44 (0)20 8688 2598
Fax +44 (0)20 7183 7186
info@filamentpublishing.com
www.filamentpublishing.com

© Wendy Howard 2014

The right of Wendy Howard to be identified as the author of this work has been asserted by her in accordance with the Designs and Copyright Act 1988.

ISBN - 978-1-910125-03-8

Printed by CreateSpace

This book is subject to international copyright and may not be copied in any way without the prior written permission of the publishers.

Dedicated to the following incredible people, and one amazing dog.

Foremost, I wish to express my deepest gratitude to my biggest supporters, my daughters; Lanna, Debra, and Tiffany. And a special thank you to my partner, Howard, for all your patience and support.

Lanna has provided inspiration, critique, and a motivational boot when needed and publishing support throughout. I don't think I could have done this without her.

Thank you to Shadow, my dearest German Shepherd, for his patience and faithfulness in waiting for his walks and being a sounding board for my ideas and many frustrations during my book writing journey.

To Lisa Tener, for her guidance in making my book a reality, and to the many people (too many to mention) who have contributed valuable input and contribution.

"People don't get what they want, because they don't know what they want."

T. Harv Eker

Contents

Part One — 15
Introduction: Let Me Be Your Personal Guide on
a Diverging Pathway — 15

Chapter One: The 7 Business Angels You Need to Meet
Who Are They? Where are They? Why Does It Matter? — 19

Chapter Two
Connecting With Your Business Angels
How does it happen? — 25

Chapter Three: Energy, the Life Force of All Living Things
Why My Dog Is Never Wrong — 29

Chapter Four: Business Chakras
Your Internal Energy Alignment — 35

Chapter Five: A Spark of Divine Light
Giving Yourself Permission To Shine — 60

Chapter Six: Meeting Your 7 Business Angels
7-Step Business Angel Plan — 63

Chapter Seven: Illuminate Your Business Heart
Lizzie's Story — 95

Part Two — 103
Chapter Eight: The New Feminine Business Economy
In Our Powerful Digital Communications Age — 105

Chapter Nine: Myths, Truths And Sand
Is Money Really Your Biggest Hurdle? — 111

Chapter Ten: Your Quirky Brain
Power Up Your Thoughts   123

Chapter Eleven: Light Up Your Amazing Soul Path
Freedom from the Veil of Illusion   133

Chapter Twelve: Your Cells Have Memories Too
David's Story   139

Chapter Thirteen: You ARE The Hero In Your Story
Awaken Your Hungry Soul   147

Chapter Fourteen: When Harry Meets Sally
Motivational Secrets in Guru Land   155

Chapter Fifteen: Your Magical Destiny Path
One Step for Mankind   161

Chapter Sixteen: Embracing Evolutionary Change
A Database in the Corridors of Time   167

Chapter Seventeen: Can You Feel It?
Shift of Universal of Consciousness   171

Chapter Eighteen: Creating the Space Where Miracles Happen
The One-Degree Shift to Change your Destiny   177

Chapter Nineteen: You Were Born a Creative Genius
Intuition, Your Fail-Safe Navigation System   185

Chapter Twenty: Evolving and Taking your Place in the World
Your Time is Now!   191

Resources   193

Holistic Business Destiny Reading   195

Introduction
Let Me Be Your Personal Guide on a Diverging Pathway

Your seven business angels are here on earth; they may already walk beside you, or they may be on another continent or place unknown to you right now. They may be right there in front of you, but it is as if you walk parallel paths. One path is paved in gold, rich in glorious bejewelled colours and bathed in the warm sunshine of life. There is a clear direction on this path, and the only signpost leads directly to riches, prosperity, and abundance. This is the path of your business angels: the path that is rightfully yours, too.

There's a parallel path that runs alongside that of your business angels' path. In comparison, it often looks bleak. It may be laden with stones or large boulders that trip you up or block your way, making it hard to progress. This is the path of confusion, of not knowing which direction to take.

Every signpost points to somewhere, but all routes lead to nowhere, and you will find yourself back at your starting point. The colours on this path are dull and greyed, like a misty morning with a hint of drizzle and a biting chill in the air. This is the path of the struggling coach, the heart-centred entrepreneur or practitioner unable to access the business prosperity path that is rightfully theirs.

You will know if you are on this parallel path. Your life and business may struggle. It's the path where hardship reigns, uncertainty flourishes, where the lifeblood of your business drains away, seeping your energy bit by bit, diluting your belief in yourself while diminishing your precious and hard-earned resources.

On this parallel path:

- You will constantly search for more leads, more sales, more clients, but it's never enough to sustain your business or the life you want.

- You will attract the wrong types of clients, those who either don't have the money to pay you or want your services for free.

- You may feel frustrated or even angry because others don't see the value in what you have to offer, despite your qualifications and hard work.

- You may feel cheated in some way that life has given you these amazing gifts and talents and then thrown you into a desert of despair where you can't find the people you know you can truly help.

- You've invested (sometimes heavily) in coaching and training courses, and you've read books galore. But still it's not working out as it should, and you're confused at what to do next.

- You know the final piece of the puzzle is still missing; it all seems a bridge too far. The gap is too wide, the distance too great.

Time is running out; your resources are stretched to the breaking point, and you desperately want that breakthrough.

There is a reason your business success has evaded you thus far. There is a reason that recognition for your work has not occurred. There is a reason you struggle when others, often offering something of less value than you, experience tremendous success. There is a reason you have so far not been richly rewarded financially for your knowledge and expertise.

The answers are right here, and by the time you finish reading *The 7 Business Angels You Need to Meet*, you will be on your way to crossing over to the lighter and plentiful path. You will soon find yourself headed in the direction of the life you cherish. You will see a signpost leading you to the riches, prosperity, and abundance you so desire for your life and business.

There's work to be done to get you onto the richly rewarding path intended for you which has been out of reach to you for far too long.
Let's begin our journey.

Let me be your guide.

> We have all a better guide
> in ourselves,
> if we would attend to it,
> than any other person can be.
> Jane Austen

Wendy Howard

Chapter One

The 7 Business Angels You Need to Meet

Who Are They? Where Are They? Why Does It Matter?

As a child I learned that I had a godmother, a special person appointed my guardian at my christening should my parents not be able to fulfil this role until I'd finally grown up and could take care of myself.

I pictured her as an amazingly beautiful tiny nymph, with sparkling, almost translucent shimmering wings as she flew around my head, waving her magical wand to grant my wishes. She reminded me of Tinkerbell, the fairy in the film Peter Pan. This seemed fitting, as I'd been named Wendy after one of the leading characters.

I recall my great disappointment at discovering my godmother was in fact my Auntie Lena, a large, overweight lady dressed head to toe in black, whom I found particularly scary in my younger years.

Arriving at Auntie Lena's house meant facing the dreaded flannel wash. She'd grab my hand, leading me over to the cold enamel sink, which was draped with a washed out flowery curtain.

She'd gleefully wipe a disgustingly smelly dishcloth over my face, neck, and hands as I closed my eyes and held my breath. I shudder at the memory, even today.

I felt cheated of the special mystical person I'd envisaged and vowed to safeguard my parents, to make sure they were still around long enough for me to grow up and take care of myself.

How does this story relate to the seven business angels?

Unlike the fictional fairy in Peter Pan, your business angels are not mystical or fantasy apparitions. They are very much real individuals here on earth. Luckily for you, though, they are not scary people like my Auntie Lena (I just thought you'd like the story). They're real people, already successful in business.

More than that, your business angels are guides and mentors with unique gifts and talents, helping heart-centred entrepreneurs share their expertise in a far greater way than if they were to do it alone.

Business angels are thought leaders and visionaries with smart entrepreneurial business acumen. They all share the traits of being connected to universal energies and have an awareness of the greater power of collaboration and synergy in the new feminine economy, illuminating the business world, and making it a better, healthier, happier and richer place for all.

Contribution through their work is extremely important to all business angels, adding value to those they work with. As you read this book you will discover the importance of your unique contribution and how each generation evolves through the contribution of the great masters at that time, scientists, authors, researchers, artists and many others. Every contribution, however small, makes a significant difference when added to the universal knowledge database, because it is all part of our evolution.

Your business angels are guides enabling you to identify and express your uniqueness, to confidently stand in your greatness and gain recognition for your contribution.

Why seven business angels?

As part of my work and during my own personal entrepreneurial journey, I've identified seven key stages of personal and business development that successful heart-centred entrepreneurs go through. And for each of the seven stages of development, there is one key person, a business angel you need to meet who has the knowledge, expertise and connections you need to grow your business at that particular step.

At each of the seven steps there are tasks to implement into your business which in turn helps to strengthen your personal chakras enabling you to overcome doubts, fears or blocks that may trip you up or cause you to struggle.

One of the problems with many businesses today, not just heart-centred ones, is that it's easy to get caught up in the whirlwind of marketing must haves, such as I must have audio, video, webinars, my own T.V. channel or the latest app for my website. Trying to keep up with technology at an ever-increasing pace is mind blowing. It causes confusion and it can end up holding you back or not knowing which direction to go in.

The thing to remember is that all marketing technologies are tactics – they're not strategy. What really matters is strategy. Once you have a strategy in place, and you know what it is that brings you alive and can feel in your heart its truly what you want to do, then begin setting out your strategy plan and only at that point look at the tactics you can apply to achieving that plan. This is the beauty of focusing on just seven key stages of the business angel plan and finding one key person as a guide for each step. It keeps it simple and the path is clear and easy to follow.

There is so much pressure on being successful that it's helpful to remind ourselves what we mean by this. What exactly is success? A definition in the Free Dictionary by Farlex is the achievement of something desired, planned, or attempted. With that in mind, we can all achieve success at whatever level we set for ourselves. You can raise the bar a little or a lot depending on what it is you want to achieve. What is your definition of personal success? Are your personal goals set against that definition? In many cases, we judge our success on how well we see others are doing, and this sets us on a path that is not our own and we easily drift off course.

To get on to the path that was intended for you, the one destiny had in mind, I've discovered there are three things that make the difference between being successful or struggling in a heart-centred business. And these three things are:

i. To have the right business skills, tools and techniques for your particular business – and to apply this know-how in the correct order. These are all learnable skills.

ii. To connect with the right people who have the knowledge and expertise to help you apply the tools and techniques in the right way, and at the time you need them. These are your business angels.

iii. The third and critical thing is that you come from a place of knowing who you are and the right destiny path for you. With that, you do the internal work to strengthen your personal energy chakras and align your business with your soul source.

Each of these three elements developed into a unique seven-stage business angel plan, make it easy for you to find and follow the success path destined for you.

My role is to help you develop your seven-step business angel plan and guide you through all seven stages of your personal and business growth, while connecting you with the relevant business angels you need to meet at each step.

As we work together I will share with you the knowledge heart-centred entrepreneurs need to know and to understand as you grow your business.

This book is just the beginning as there is a lot to learn, and my hope is that you will gain a deeper knowledge and insight into the greater universal perspective and how to apply the business angel philosophy to grow your heart-centred business.

> # Sometimes the heart sees what is invisible to the eye.
>
> ## H. Jackson Brown, Jr.

Wendy Howard

The best and most
beautiful things
in the world cannot
be seen or even touched -
they must be felt
with the heart.

Helen Keller

Chapter Two

Connecting With Your Business Angels How does it happen?

You may be networking like crazy, talking to everyone and anyone around you, have built your website, delved into social networking, taken numerous self-development courses and are seemingly doing all the right things, but still, it's not working out as you'd planned. Can you relate to that?

There's a reason for this.

It's easy to get caught up in what the majority of other people are doing, and get the feeling that it's the right thing to do for your business too. For instance: I can recall for the first few years in my business attending numerous networking meetings. It took a lot of effort to attend regularly, and it cost time and money to be there. I discovered the majority of people were on the same level that I was at during that time, and attending for the same reason, to find more clients and make their business effort worthwhile. I was no different but I knew there had to be a better and easier way, which is why I'm sharing what I discovered with you now.

I learned that if you are not communicating from soul level in your business, you will not be giving out the right messages to attract your audience. No matter how much you say or however loud you shout, your message will not resonate with the people you want to attract.

In turn, when you are out of alignment with the soul source of your business, you will not be emitting the energy frequency or making the right connections with the people who will help you to grow, namely your business angels.

Your business angels are visionaries, change masters, knowledgeable, sensitive and here on this earth to help you realize your signature genius and live to your highest potential but there is something very important in how they connect with you. They emit a higher energy frequency, which is only picked up on an intuitive or knowing level and you have to be open to receiving that.

When I made this realization, I started to move in different circles and to meet people who really made a difference in my life. Connections came from all parts of the world. I began to use my intuition and to align myself with this higher energy frequency. I became much calmer and my life and work much more fulfilling. It was only then that I found I could let go of that which had been holding me back, and began on the path that was always intended for me, but I hadn't been able to see it until that point. Like a foggy morning the route ahead was misted over.

Without an energy alignment, your call for help will not be picked up at the time you need it to be, or indeed your business angels will instinctively know you are not ready to work with them, so they won't step out. Believe me, this happens.

Think of it like this, for instance: when all the circuitry in your house is connected, you have light, you have heat; you have a power source at your fingertips. The power source is invisible as you can't see it but you know it is there because the connection is clear and strong. The lights glow and all you appliances work.

Similarly in your business, if the intuitive circuitry is connected up, you are aligned soul to soul in your work, your message will be strong and resonate with the people you want to attract.

You will naturally emit a higher energy frequency and attract your business angels, the mentors meant to help you on your business soul journey. You will instantly know and feel they are the right connection for you.

The circuitry you rely on is not an electrical circuit board as in your home, but rather your brain. The connection between you and your business angels happens on an intuitive level and this communication is via the limbic (emotional) part of the brain, which does not have words, it has feelings. This is explained in detail in Chapter Ten: Your Quirky Brain.

Working with your business angels is a very special relationship because as you join your unique light with theirs, you will be illuminating our amazing world with ease. Your message will be heard and heartwarmingly felt. Your invitation will extend to as many people as you are able to help, who in return will want to follow YOU. You will luxuriate in the wonderful place of personal power, humility and fulfillment.

This is far removed from being wrapped up in the physical world or being caught up in the loop of overwhelm, hard work, and stress. Staying in that place, on that 'other' path, you will not get the breakthrough or results you want. Similarly to having a power cut, your connection to the abundant universal supply will be cut off and fused out.

Your business angels are there to shift you out of the loop of overwhelm and to step into your true greatness so you can take your place in the world and become who you are meant to be. When this happens, everything flows; all the unique pieces of your success path fall into place.

Before we go through each step of your business angel plan and the profiles of each business angel, let's gain an understanding of the importance of energy as the life force of all living things and discover the third success element which includes your seven energy chakras and how they relate to your business.

> There is no logical
> way to the discovery of
> these elemental laws.
> There is only the way
> of intuition,
> which is helped by
> a feeling for the order
> lying behind the appearance.
>
> Albert Einstein

Chapter Three

Energy, the Life Force of All Living Things

Why My Dog Is Never Wrong

Have you ever walked into a building and sensed the history of the people who once lived there? Or picked up an object or a piece of jewellery and instantly felt a connection with its previous owner or wearer?

The practice of psychometry, where energy is stored within objects, is not uncommon, as is walking into a building and sensing occupants from the past. I've certainly experienced this myself on numerous occasions.

It's the life force of all living things: chi. Subtle energy, known as chi or qi, has been used for thousands of years, particularly in China. Chi can be considered as the 'life force' of all living things and may become imprinted on inanimate objects, including properties.

Recently, on returning home from our walk with my German Shepherd, Shadow, I sensed someone had been in my home the minute I reached my front drive.

Shadow could sense it too. He immediately perked up, his ears perched on high alert and exuberant energy coursed throughout his body. This, in dog terms, indicates the energy is good and familiar.

Once I'd let him off the lead and opened my back door, he excitedly bounded through my home in expectation of a welcome visitor, searching the floor with his nose down and eventually ending up sitting by the front door, alert with tail wagging. But there was no one there.

I instinctively knew the visitor had been my daughter Lanna, and Shadow knew this too. Although he could not tell me in actual words, his knowledge of events was very clear. Sure enough Lanna called me later that same day telling me she'd dropped by, but as I wasn't at home, she'd decided to leave after a few minutes. We have the ability to pick up energy instinctively and to feel if it is good or bad.

Animals have a natural instinct for using subtle intuitive energy and instantly know if it's favourable or not. They do not question or seek to prove its existence as often is the case for humans. Animals accept what is, and Shadow clearly does this well.

Another time while having a new kitchen fitted, Shadow took an instant dislike to the plumber's young apprentice.

Showing his distaste, he took refuge in the garden, refusing to enter the house while the young apprentice was in my home. Shadow's body language told me exactly how he felt: head held down almost to the ground, ears flat against his head, tail curled up and tucked under his back legs. This was Shadow's way of telling me he didn't trust this person, didn't like him, and wanted to get him out of his home, which I did at the earliest convenient time. I later learned this person was on probation for theft and aggressive behaviour with intent.

Animals and many humans, including your finely tuned business angels are highly sensitive to the existence and power of subtle energy. Lets look at the scientific research on the power of energy.

Chi energy is a fundamental aspect of many practices we take for granted, including tai chi, qigong (chigung), yoga, martial arts, energy healing, and Reiki. Natural healers and complementary therapists regularly use chi to assist clients restoring their physical or mental health towards optimum level.

At an individual level, the key principle is 'Chi follows intention'. If you focus on a particular part of your body, you can, with practice, affect temperature and sensitivity to that part of your body, as well as remove pain and accelerate healing.

At a business level, energy flows where attention goes, accelerating growth and income. If you focus on a particular area of your business, you will for instance, gain a deeper sensitivity to the true needs of your client group. You will remove the pain of feast or famine, and accelerate growth and income by energising the relevant growth areas.

Chi is affected by conscious and subconscious thought. As such, it is used to distantly restore personal health issues or improve the 'atmosphere' of a building. In some cases, verbal or visual communication may not be required between the healer and person or place to be healed, either before or during the session or process.

Wendy Howard

Energy healing without boundaries.

The effective distance of healing energy appears to be without limits. Experiments have been documented over thousands of miles. The Intention Experiment by Lynne McTaggart documented amazing changes taking place in many parts of the world using the power of mass intention under strict scientific experiment conditions. You can join in some of these experiments online at http://theintentionexperiment.com

I found particularly interesting Lynne's chapter on healing as well as ideas on super radiance and the studies on light bodies. Lynne explains that every living thing emits photons, waves of light so small they are invisible to the human eye. For instance; much of the light emanating from distant stars in the sky has been travelling for millions of years. Starlight contains a star's individual history. Even if a star has died long before it's light reached the earth, its information remains, as an indelible footprint in the sky. Imagine for a moment what this means, and you can almost picture yourself emitting invisible biophotons that will travel on carrying your history throughout time.

Some technologies can show a representation of the chi energy changing in real time as people interact or consciously control their own thoughts and focus. A standard kinesiology (muscle testing) demonstration appears to indicate a dramatic strengthening or weakening of a subject's muscles on demand by the effect of focused thoughts from an audience.

Chi can be seen around living things in the form of the human aura. Krishna Madappa, an Indian mystic and scientist, teamed up with Russian physicists to develop the world's first 3D human aura imaging technology and computer software.

With this new science and technology, it is possible to not only see a Kirlian-type image of the whole human body and aura, but also to map the real data or information inside of the human aura.

Russian scientist Professor Konstantin Korotkov's patented bioelectrography device (GDV – Gas Discharge Visualization, May 2012) captures living energy fields around people, plants and water, all living systems. In doing so, the GDV machine can measure altered states of consciousness, chakra energy amplitude and alignment, vital signs and energy integration. You can watch a video explaining about this technology here: http://www.youtube.com/watch?v=DhBYqkos-Xk

The GDV technology can be used for early detection of cancer, heart disease and other medical conditions. It can measure the energy in water and how consciousness affects it. For instance, it has been documented that chemical changes occur when water is blessed by a holy-leader. Why this should occur can be somewhat explained in the amazing film, Water, the Great Mystery, where science has made a quantum leap in understanding how mind can be recorded by the most simple element in nature (water) and on the periodic table: H20. The film explores that if water had memory, and its main component being hydrogen, then the whole universe would have memory. Hydrogen was born between 100 and 1,000 seconds after the big bang. It makes up 75% of the known mass of the universe and now, is part of the missing equation. Source: http://topdocumentaryfilms.com/water-great-mystery

Energy changes in your aura can be measured to the second using this more advanced GDV technology, whereas Kirlian photography can only capture one second of a human aura and does not measure real data.

What is very exciting about this technology is that it can prove and show real data about the existence and functions of consciousness, and the human soul. For instance: Konstantin Korotkov captured the timing of astral disembodiment in which the spirit leaves the body at the moment of death with a bioelectrographic camera.
Source:http://consciouslifenews.com/scientist-photographs-soul-leaving-body/#

Healing energy in business today.

What is very special and different about energy work, or 'energy medicine' as it is sometimes referred to, is that it can positively address every aspect of a personal and business situation.

Your deepest intentions shape the direction of your life and your business. It's your reaction to any circumstance that is the fundamental cause of any stress, anger, relationship issue, confidence, lack of business success, or many health issues you may be experiencing.

I'm sure you'll agree whether you choose to delve into the vaults of scientific evidence, which makes fascinating reading, or trust the instinct of your dog, as I do with Shadow, energy connections and sensitivity to energy is extremely important to achieving a positive outcome.

Emitting a positive energy frequency to attract the right people, your business angels, combined with the right actions and business acumen will go a long way to guaranteeing your success in whatever you choose to do.

Now, after this heavy session on energy, lets lighten up, and have some fun as we get into the business chakras and understanding the part they play in growing a successful heart-centred business.

Chapter Four

Business Chakras
Your Internal Energy Alignment

This chapter focuses primarily on the amazing work of Dr Lisa Turner of www.psycademy.com and I am very grateful for her contribution in this respect.

Stepping onto the path of the heart-centred, spiritual entrepreneur, many fears are likely to arise: asking for money, speaking out, stepping up, and becoming visible can all feel scary.

At times, it feels easier to drop out before you achieve success. Or you may become paralysed by fear of being shot down, wanting to remain hidden behind the real 'you' in your safe but small world. Being small is fine, if this is your choice. But it's not fine if you're in fear, hiding behind the real you.

To fulfill your purpose and mission, there's also the internal work required. Imagine an iceberg. Approximately ten percent of the iceberg is visible above the water, which you can clearly see. This is the physical part.

There's another 90 percent below the surface. This is the invisible part, which you cannot see but you know it's there. This 90 percent represents your emotional, mental, and spiritual aspects, where your unique thoughts, feelings, motivational drives and values decide your action subconsciously.

The Iceberg Analogy
Physical, Mental, Emotional, and Spiritual Realms

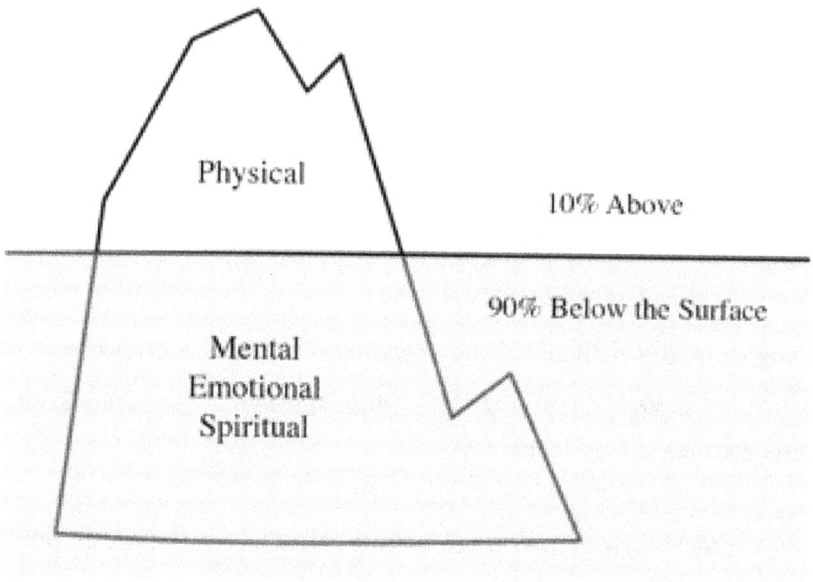

The 90% below the surface is invisible, but you know it is there. Here lies your feelings, motivational drives and values, which manifest into your thoughts that drive your behaviour and the actions you decide to take in your life. It is your psychological blueprint.

By being awakened and called to service, but refusing to own it, you are doing a disservice not only to yourself but also to the world. The heart-centred entrepreneur's calling comes from the praise of people who are seeking the solution you have to offer that will solve their particular problem. You must stand your ground, honour your contribution and own your greatness.

When you are a soul-driven heart-centred entrepreneur, your business is a reflection of your unique purpose, perception, and personal power.

You must own this 100 percent. To be truly confident to stand in your power, you can do this by strengthening your chakras.

Chakra means Wheel of Light, spinning vortexes of energy contained in each individual person. To help you gain clarity on the chakras in business, I turned to specialist Dr. Lisa Turner, known as the "Psychic Scientist."

What is a Chakra?

In Lisa's words:
"Okay, what is a chakra? In the physical body it comes from the East Indian tradition and it is an energy centre, which doesn't actually exist!"

As an engineer, I'm happy with something that doesn't exist because what we've got are complex numbers. A complex number is a number that doesn't exist. A complex number contains an imaginary component. So we pretend they exist and they are pretty useful. So that's pretty much what a chakra is. It doesn't physically exist, but it's pretty useful as a model that explains our existence, our business, and our personality traits, etc.

Science has now identified that there are nerve clusters, nerve ganglions, which exist in the parts of the body, which relate to those identified chakra personality traits.

This is part of evolution. Thinking in terms of this as a model is useful. As an engineer, we use models, which are useful, give or take ten percent. Imagine if you could have everything in your life with a plus or a minus ten percent. Would you be okay with that, or not? It's just a model. Believe it.

So chakras are energy centres that relate to the body and have a quality of energy. They are located on the midline of the body.

There are seven in total, and they govern the psychological properties. Higher chakras are our mental side, and the chakras on the lower part of the body are our instinctive side. Similarly, chakras are centres of energy in your business."

Let's go through each of the business chakras to discover what you can expect when all is well and what happens when it's not working well.

1. Crown Chakra

The crown chakra is located at the top of your head. It relates to higher power and spirituality. In relation to your business, most businesses start with an idea or a flash of inspiration. Your crown chakra is the gateway.

Crown Chakra: Activated, Open, and Working

- You will know what your purpose is, what your mission is, and what your business is all about.
- Your business will be a joyful expression of your life purpose.
- Taking time out of your business will prove easy, as there's a void to let inspiration and creativity in.
- You have confidence, even in the face of negative people who doubt or question what you do.
- You will have easy access to the super conscious.

Signs Your Crown Chakra Is Not Working Well

- You know deep inside you've got a purpose, but you're not sure what that is.
- You want to start out on your own, but you're still doing a day job to support yourself.

- You are trying to fit your purpose into a business rather than fit your business into your purpose.
- You may have joined someone else's business, rather than going it alone.
- You may be involved in multiple things at once, so you're not focused on anything in particular.
- You will face a lot of conflict and dissatisfaction and have feelings that 'there must be more than this'.
- You feel bogged down in the minutae of day-to-day business, unable to break free or to find the space to be you.

Crown Chakra-Related Emotion and State

Emotion:
Attachment, devotion, trust, loss of meaning or identity, selflessness, values, ethics.

State: The right to know

Spiritual Lesson:
Intuitive knowing, living in the NOW

Associated Colour:
Violet/White

Gemstone:
Amber, Diamond, Star Tulip

NOTE: In business, it's important to get this chakra open and working first; then go down to the next chakra. There is a structure and order to follow.

2. Third Eye or Intuitive Vision Chakra

What started out as an idea in your crown chakra now becomes a clear vision about what it is you want your business to look like and what you want it to do.

Third Eye (Intuitive Vision) Chakra: Activated, Open, and Working

- Thinking through ideas comes easily, and you will have inspired solutions that give you what you want.
- You are wise, including being wise enough to ask for support when you need it.
- You can think clearly and see what lies ahead and the path you must follow.
- It's very obvious who your karmic clients are. You will naturally be attracted to your karmic (kindred) spirits.
- When you meet your business kindred spirits (business angels), you will instinctively know this when you meet them. You will feel comforted and connected at soul level, regardless of where they are in the world.

Signs Your Third Eye (Intuitive Vision) Chakra Is Not Working Well

- You will at times have complete brain fog, where you don't find solutions to problems.
- Thoughts go round and round in your head, and you find yourself thinking the same thought and coming back to the same place, without any solution or end in sight.
- Confused as to who your karmic clients are.
- You don't know what your niche or specialty is.
- You will be easily distracted by bright, shiny objects or the next best thing.
- You are prone to taking on projects that seem like good ideas at the time, but often turn out to be big distractions or blocks.
- You may be such a big thinker that clear thought doesn't come down to a clear vision, so there's no path to follow to make it happen.
- You won't immediately recognise your business kindred spirits (business angels), so you miss out on opportunities.
- Your ideas don't go any further than the idea stage; they never get off the starting block.

Third Eye (Intuitive Vision) Chakra-Related Emotion and State

Emotion: Illusion, fear of truth, evaluation, concept of reality, emotional intelligence.

State: The right to see.

Spiritual Lesson: Understanding, reality check, detachment, open mind.

Associated Colour: Indigo

Gemstone: Purple Flourite, Sugarlite, Lapis.

> The more you trust your intuition, the more empowered you become, the stronger you become, and the happier you become.
> Gisele Bundchen

3. Throat Chakra

The throat chakra is your communication, listening and understanding chakra.

Throat Chakra: Activated, Open, and Working

- People will immediately get a clear understanding of what you do and relate to what you are saying.
- Your sales and marketing messages will be working and converting into sales.
- Your message will resonate soul to soul, heart to heart.
- You find it easy to ask for money.
- You will be really clear on what people are saying to you. Communication is great.
- You are completely at ease speaking about what you do and how you help people.

Signs Your Throat Chakra Is Not Working Well

- You find it difficult asking for money and don't like asking people to pay your fees.
- You may find that people have manipulated or lied to you because you can't see through the veil of their illusion.
- You feel tongue tied when you speak or don't know what to say in certain situations.
- People are confused when you try to explain what it is you do; there's a lot of confusion.

Throat Chakra
Related Emotion and State

Emotion: Personal expression, creativity, faith, decision making, addiction, lies, lack of connection, confusion.

State: The right to speak and hear truth.

Spiritual Lesson:
Confession, faith, truthfulness over deceit.

Associated Colour:
Sky Blue.

Gemstone:
Chrysocolla, Lapis, Blue Opal.

4. The Heart Chakra

The heart chakra, as you would expect, is situated in the centre of the chest. It's really important, especially for heart-centred businesses. The heart chakra is about giving, but it is also about receiving.

Heart Chakra: Activated, Open and Working

- You will ask for and get the fees you want, and you will know you deserve them.
- You can quickly and easily see who your ideal client is (and who isn't).
- You feel completely at ease and abundant in your work and in life.
- You know your true value and worth.

Signs Your Heart Chakra Is Not Working Well

- One of the main signs your heart chakra is blocked is that you are giving, giving, and giving; but getting little or nothing back in return.
- Others tend to use you, taking your goodness for granted but not placing value on what you have given them.
- You may feel resentment for your having so much to give but not receiving anything back in return.
- You may experience anger or frustration at having worked hard for qualifications when not reaping the rewards from your achievements.

Heart Chakra-Related Emotion and State

Emotion: Love, compassion, generosity, hurt, rejection, sorrow, resentment, hate, envy, jealousy.

State: The right to love and be loved.

Spiritual Lesson: Love, Forgiveness, Compassion

Heart Chakra: Forgiveness, unconditional love, letting go, trust, compassion

Associated Colour: Green.

Gemstone: Malachite, Emerald, Rose Quartz.

5. Solar Plexus Chakra

Your solar plexus is your power chakra. In business, it is the fuel driving your business. It is your passion, your motivation. It is also your leadership.

Solar Plexus Chakra: Activated, Open, and Working

- You will have the drive and motivation to be inspired. You will be in your power.
- You will be able to focus on a task with total concentration and without getting distracted.
- When you start something, you will be able to finish it. You won't be thrown off course while you do it.
- You have great business boundaries, so when someone says to you, 'Can I have this extra thing from you?', you can say, 'Actually, that's not going to work for me, but thanks for asking', and people will respect that.
- You will demonstrate great leadership and have sound business boundaries.

Signs Your Solar Plexus Chakra Is Not Working Well

- You are disorganised, and everything is chaotic.
- You will start tasks but not finish them.
- You'll procrastinate; people will be stealing your time and draining your energy.
- You find yourself saying 'yes' to things you don't really want to do.
- If you have a team, you won't be leading them well. Your team won't be supportive of you. You will find yourself doing more for the team than they are doing for you.

Solar Plexus Chakra-Related Emotion and State

Emotion: Self-esteem, fear of rejection, self-image fears, indecisiveness, fear of secrets being found out.

State: The right to feel.

Spiritual Lesson: Acceptance of oneself in the life stream, self-love.

Associated Colour: Yellow

Gemstone: Jasper, Golden Topaz, Yellow Tourmaline

6. Sacral Chakra

What's the role of sex in business? Well, the sexy sacral chakra is all about desire, lust, reproduction and production. There is a lot of movement and creativity in all senses as a major function of the sacral chakra.

Emotions are energy in motion. If they are not expressed, the energy is repressed. As energy, it has to go somewhere. Emotional energy moves us, as does all energy. To deny emotion is to deny the vital energy of life.

Sacral Chakra: Activated, Open, and Working

- You will arouse desire in your prospects for your products and services.
- Your website will attract attention, and people will be signing up for your online information.
- You will get noticed, and people will want what you're offering.
- You will be flexible in taking the time to find out what your prospects desire and want before taking the time to fulfill that desire.

The sacral chakra is a bit like the film *When Harry Met Sally* and the part when she was faking an orgasm, and the other woman sitting at a table in another part of the restaurant said to the waiter waiting for her order, 'I'll have what she's having'. It's an attraction like that.

Signs Your Sacral Chakra Is Not Working Well

- You've got a website, but it's not working for you.
- You're marketing, but it doesn't attract desire. It just falls flat.
- People respond by saying, 'That's nice', but they don't buy. They'll go away and think about it, but don't come back.
- There is no wow factor of 'I want that' happening.
- You struggle to focus on a project. It may be that you are overactive and it's not happening.
- You may be overly rigid, such as thinking you are the only one who can do certain activities in your business.
- You may be inflexible in your approach, such as working very set days or hours and not offering any alternatives.
- You don't have a balance of boundaries and desire, such as offering what people want and giving them alternative ways of working with you.

Sacral Chakra	Related Emotion and State
Emotion:	Power, guilt, blame, control, morality.
State:	Emotional flow.
Spiritual Lesson:	Creativity, manifestation, learning to let go.
Associated Colour:	Orange.
Gemstones:	Garnet, Moonstone, Orange Tourmaline.

7. Base Chakra

The base chakra is your money chakra. It is right at the base of your body. It faces and points towards the earth, whereas the sacral chakra points upwards towards the sky.

Base Chakra: Activated, Open, and Working

- You will have money coming in, as you've given birth to the idea, which is coming to fruition.
- You manage your time well and will have built a team or virtual team around you as support.
- Your physical environment is beautiful and pleasurable for working in.
- There is a healthy balance of wealth and time in your life and business.

Signs Your Base Chakra Is Not Working Well

- You feel trapped in the situation of having no money coming in, but you can't afford to pay for the help and support you need.
- You may need training, but can't afford to pay for it or to find the time to fit training in to your schedule.
- You try to sell your ideas or want someone else to do the work for you.
- You give your ideas away, don't see value in them or know how to monetise the idea.
- Your environment is unpleasant, chaotic, and not conducive to your well-being.
- Nothing is working out for you or going anywhere.

Base Chakra-Related Emotion and State

Emotion: Fear, blind panic, survival, security, social order, family.

State: The right to be here.

Spiritual Lesson: Material world lessons.

Associated Colour: Red.

Gemstones: Haematite, Black Tourmaline, Onyx.

Exercises to Clear Your Chakras

Exercise One
Release the Emotion

By not dealing with an emotional upset, trauma, or painful experience when it occurs, it will resurface as emotional toxicity, showing up in areas of life such as insomnia, illness, depression, anxiety, and other issues.

As a heart-centred business owner, this will be reflected as difficulties or blocks in your business, preventing growth and income.

Spiritual leader Deepak Chopra suggests by turning to our inherent intelligence, harmony, and creativity, we can create a positive outcome. This can be achieved by using a combination of meditation, diet, exercise, and sleep. Deepak suggests a seven-step exercise to release emotions which includes the following elements:

Step One: Identifying and locating the emotion physically.

Take a few quiet moments to meditate in silence. Identify with the emotional upset. Give the incident a word to describe what you are feeling. Give the feeling a name. What one word epitomises the painful experience? Focus your attention on this word.

Step Two: Witness the experience.

Gradually allow your attention to move away from the word and into your body. The two elements of an idea in your mind and a physical sensation in your body make up an emotion. We feel emotion in our bodies. Identify where in the body you are feeling the emotional experience.

Step Three: Express the emotion.

Place your hand on the part of your body where you are feeling pain. You may have more than one body part which is feeling the hurt; identify these parts. As you do this, place your hand on that part of the body and say for instance, "It hurts here, in my heart."

Every cell in your body knows what is unbalanced and will be feeling pain physically, mentally, or spiritually. By identifying and befriending the sensations and the wisdom stored there, the pain is leading you towards wholeness.

Writing something down on paper helps too. When I was going through a particularly traumatic time in my life, I kept a diary. I wrote down my feelings using whatever words I felt. It was a great healer. Reading this back later on in my life, I can see how far I've come. I'm very proud of that.

Step Four: Take responsibility for your feelings.

This gives you the power to make the pain melt away. You no longer blame anyone else for having caused your pain, so you no longer have to depend on anyone else to make it go away. Hold on to this consciousness for a few moments.

Step Five: Share the outcome.

Activate the new pattern of behaviour after the old painful pattern is released. Deepak says this is important. He suggests that you imagine speaking with the person who was involved in that original painful experience. What would you say to them now?

As you do this, remember that this person was not the real cause of your pain. The real cause of your pain was your response to the incident. In your transformed state, you are now free.

Step Six: Anchoring.

The process of anchoring is an effective way to solidify the learning experience. It can be as simple as touching a place on your wrist or leg to bring back associated good feelings. Take a few moments to close your eyes and focus on how good it feels to take responsibility and to be free.

Is the feeling strong? Focus on this feeling making it as strong and real as possible. While you do this touch your wrist or leg and begin to associate the good feeling with that touch. This is a technique you can use anytime, anywhere.

Step Seven: Celebrate.

Feel gratitude and celebrate the painful experience that has taken place as being valuable material that has helped you move to a higher level of consciousness.

What was previously a disconnected, destructive, and disabled part of your psyche is now integrated and contributing its power towards wholeness and spiritual transformation.

Celebrate by going out with friends, having dinner out, or give yourself a special treat. Celebrate the renewed and freer you.

> A man can fail many times, but he isn't a failure until he begins to blame somebody else.
>
> John Burroughs

Exercise Two

Exercise the Behaviour Associated with the Relevant Chakra

Begin by identifying where the emotional pain is and the part of your body associated with the pain. You can determine which chakra is affected by examining where the difficulties in your life or business are, which are not bringing you the results and rewards you want.

After identifying the chakra that needs activating, you then plan an activity, which will cause you to activate and clear that particular chakra.

For instance, if it's your throat chakra that needs activating, start talking to people. Start sharing what it is you do and begin to listen deeply to the responses you receive in return. Increase your communication. Go out and meet people.

By increasing your communication, raising energy, connecting, and releasing pent up emotions, you are clearing the relevant chakra.

Exercise Three
Energy Clearing Session

Have a one-on-one session with a guided energy practitioner. An energy clearing session involves completing an in-depth questionnaire, followed by a conversation. When the time is right, the practitioner will perform a healing session on the relevant chakras.

I share my personal experience of an energy clearing session in the Energy Business Angel section in Chapter Six.

Note: I'd like to extend my greatest thanks and gratitude to Dr. Lisa Turner for her generous contribution to this particular chapter. To find about Lisa's work visit www.psycademy.com

> Painful as it may be,
> a significant emotional
> event can be the
> catalyst for choosing
> a direction that serves us -
> and those around us -
> more effectively.
> Look for the learning.
>
> Louisa May Alcott

Chapter Five

A Spark of Divine Light
Giving Yourself Permission To Shine

I'll begin by sharing with you the story of Tikum Olam, which comes from the world of Jewish mysticism meaning to heal the world.

Basically, Tikum Olam means that the world has been broken into many pieces, similar to a large jigsaw puzzle. Each piece of the puzzle is a spark of divine light.

Amid the chaos, sadness, and brokenness of our world, it is your job - everyone's job - to put the pieces of the puzzle back together again. Until all the pieces of divine light are in place, the work of creation will not be complete.

I take the view that we can all add our unique piece of divine light to the universal puzzle on our personal life's journey, no matter how small our contribution.

There is no better way of doing this than through work that resonates with your soul and by giving yourself permission to shine - not holding back or waiting for 'one day' when you will ... because that won't happen.

By making your contribution you are adding to the knowledge of the great masters who have gone before. In doing so, your life has meaning and you enjoy the work that is entirely right for you. The greater financial rewards of your work enable you to help more people. It is putting into practice the universal law of giving and receiving, and the law of polarity.

Building your business with the help of business angels attracts the right people to help you, enabling you to grow your business aligned with your soul purpose and who you were meant to be.

There are a few key points to consider before we look closer at the input your business requires from each of the seven business angels and you can begin to set out your seven step business angel plan.

Key Point 1
Setting out your business angel plan requires you to engage with just one key business angel at each stage and to benefit from their individual expertise and input.

Key Point 2
There are actions to take at each step of your business angel plan and I'm sure you will experience a few 'aha' moments as you begin implement the actions into your business.

Key Point 3
When you begin working on your business angel plan there is a natural overlap and synergy because nothing works in isolation.

Everything is connected and collaboration is key. Business angels may work together at any given time on your business angel plan.

Key Point 4

Your particular business angels will differ according to your business needs and future desires and how you are drawn to working together. If it feels right for you, that's the person to work with.

Key Point 5

Depending on your particular specialism, expertise and knowledge, you may wish to undertake a number of tasks on your business angel plan by yourself. Keep it simple. Follow each step in sequence.

Let's get started on your business angel plan and identify the seven business angels you need to meet, and their input to ensure your business success.

> "Listen to the sweet longing that sings from your heart. It sings your life song. What is it that you most long to do?"
>
> Barbara Brennan,
> 'Seeds of the Spirit'

Chapter Six

Meeting Your 7 Business Angels
7-Step Business Angel Plan

Your business angel plan has seven steps for you to work through. At each step you will need to seek out the business angel who will teach you the lesson you need to learn.

Step One: Concept Business Angel
Related Chakra: Crown
Lesson: Finding your Signature Genius

Begin your journey on the sacred angel path by seeking out the business angel who will bring complete clarity about your purpose, your mission, and what your business is about. It's the first critical step to aligning your soul with your business.

Julie Ann Turner, Founder and CEO of Creator's Guide, says you have to start with your greatness. Become clear on your vision and crystal clear about your own signature genius.

People start in the wrong place by looking at the next promotion, the next media message, the next email. But if you are not starting out from your unique greatness, you will not stand out.

What is your greatness?
What is your artistry?
What are your superhero qualities?

You are the only one who can share that. It is your signature genius, your unique greatness. That is what you need to go back to; tap into your childhood dreams. Identify with who you were meant to be before life got in the way. When you do that, you will rediscover your inner awareness.

When you step into your greatness, you instantly know it. You are full of happiness, serving people at their highest value. When you are clear about your signature genius, it will be bigger and clearer than you ever imagined. Stepping up and out will be scary at first. It does take courage, but your growth will be incredible.

You will meet different thought leaders and visionaries along the way. You need to connect with people who are just a little way ahead of you, rather than being so far ahead you can't see the path. When you are creating something new to bring out your uniqueness and to formulate what that is, you need to work with someone who has already carved it out.

You must remember that you are not alone. Your sisters and brothers are all around the world, and they are stepping up to meet you. They are your kindred spirits. Your guide needs to be someone who will not tell you how great they are, but someone who is there to remind you just how great you are.

There is a step-by-step sequence that all top leaders and visionaries follow, and it begins with that vision - moving from what is to what can be. The key is to shift into that vision. Who am I? Who am I meant to serve?

In the wise words of Julie Ann, "The power is not out there. It's already in you. So start with getting the guidance to find that greatness that is already there. It's time to stop looking and start finding what is already there."

Your Concept Business Angel will help to formulate your idea and identify who you were meant to be at soul level.

Exercise:

Ask a close family member, a parent, a sibling or relative what was special about you when you were child. Explore what you loved to do.

What were your early dreams?

What happened to those dreams?

Did you develop them or forget them?

If you could re-write your life story what would it be?

What would you be doing?

Who would you be with?

Where would you live?

What would bring you fulfillment? Write this down.

Go back to the person you asked the original question to and explore who you were always meant to be.

This is your first business angel.

Step 2: Clarity Business Angel
Related Chakra: Intuitive Vision
Lesson: Clarity, Creativity and Strategy

Your second step is in making a transition from the idea floating around in your head into creativity and strategy giving you clarity, direction and focus. In order to reach your vision, it has to be broken down into tangible, do-able steps, and packaged to make the profit you want by serving your clients; and in doing so, earning the income you desire and deserve.

Your clarity business angel has the ability to tap into your vision, and help you put together your ideal product or service. Then help you plan your action steps to achieve your goals. This is a creative and fun stage, full of possibilities and its very much like going on a treasure hunt for the pot of gold.

Imagine for a few moments you're sailing the high Caribbean seas, with the glorious sunshine beaming down, as you sail towards the island where the treasure you seek lies.

There are pirates hell-bent on sabotaging your success. You have a precious map with a cross in the centre, and you have to decipher secret codes written into that map, picking out the clues to decide on your actions.

Eventually, you find that place where the treasure is buried, indicated by a cross on your map.

Taking out your spade, you dig deep into the sandy ground. It doesn't take long - and then you find it.

It's an old wooden chest, remarkably intact considering the time it's spent waiting for you to arrive with the golden key. You place the key in the lock, your hands trembling in anticipation; the key turns, the lid springs open, and there it is: the treasure you've sought for so long.

But there's a rumble in the distance. Pirates are hot on your heels, breaking through the trees, clambering over the stony ground, rifles and swords at the ready. You must make a quick escape with your treasure. After all your efforts, you so deserve to keep the treasure. It will change your life forever.

The race back to your ship begins. Adrenaline flowing, your fellow guides help and protect you, but you know it depends on your actions as to whether or not you succeed in your mission.

Bravely overcoming all obstacles, taking the shortest and safest route possible, your guides by your side, deferring any distractions, you reach the sanctuary of your ship.

Your sailing vessel is far superior to that of any pirate. It is designed that way by experts; it has a speed others only dream about.

The home run is a breeze. Your loved ones welcome you back, knowing their future is assured by your heroic efforts and the treasure you have with you.

Your fellow guides wave you a final farewell as they sail into the sunset, knowing their job is done. It has all worked out just as it should.

Your Clarity Business Angel is your creative guide, identifying the hidden treasure in your business and setting out the map to direct you to your treasure.

They will identify the easiest route for you and the vessel (business model) you must take. They will flag up the danger points and costly mistakes you must avoid on your journey. They will introduce you to known and trusted advisers as and when you need them.

At this early stage, negativity and doubt demons may rise up from your subconscious mind, knocking your confidence, wanting to suck you into the dark seas of despair. You have to let go of doubts and fears. This is your journey to self-belief and receiving what is justifiably yours.

Distractions may appear as bright shiny objects, good ideas which seem brilliant at the time but actually throw you down another route. These need to be ignored. Your map will hold your focus.

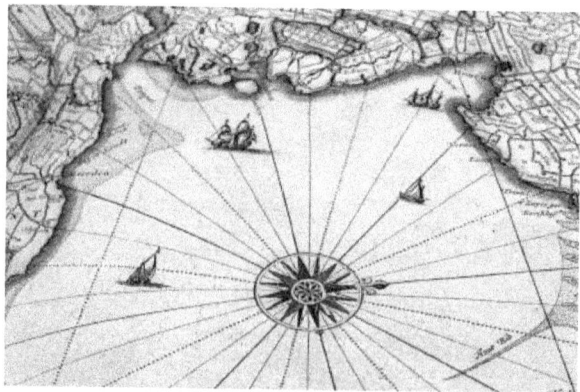

You need a strong guide who already knows the territory and will keep you focused on the map, diverting distractions and keeping your motivation high.

Your map will include detailed planning for each of the seven steps so you know exactly what to do at each stage. A profile of the business angels will be identified so the relevant skills are brought into your business at exactly the right time you need them. There will be a number of red flags that act as warnings, or blue flags for obstacles or likely challenges.

Exercise:

Start with the end in mind.

What is it you want to achieve?

What does it look like?

How much income do you want to have?

How will this make you feel?

How will it improve your life?

Set out a plan for the next 12 months and work backwards month-by-month, right back to actions you will take today.

Ideally your Clarity Business Angel will be a business coach who specialises in creativity and transformation with the ability to map out your plan step-by-step with you. Your map will help you to maintain focus, keep you on track and avoid those mishaps.

To book a unique Business Destiny Reading go to www.spiritofvenus.co.uk/businessdestinyreading or to spend a Creativity & Business Transformational Day working on your business visit www.7businessangels.com

Step 3: Media Business Angel
Related Chakra: Throat
Lesson: Core story, articulate your Message

The lesson your media business angel brings is in knowing how to tell your story and voice your message in words that will resonate with your prospective clients. This is the step where you will articulate your core story and unique message when speaking, writing your website copy, making videos, webinars and any other promotional method with words that will subconsciously seep into the realms of your prospect's brains, creating the desire for your products or services.

In Chapter Ten you will discover the quirky ways in which your brain works and transmits messages. Your messages are first of all filtered by the reptilian or croc brain. It determines whether or not your prospect should consider your message at all. The croc brain says, 'Is it a threat?', 'Do I kill it, eat it, mate with it, or all three?' or 'Can I do without it?'.

Your brain is likely to discard anything that is not exciting, dangerous, or new. Communication is key as to whether or not your business message ever gets heard at all.

Your communication must be concise and congruent with who you are and what the outcome will be for your prospect. Your communication, whether it's through your website, brochures, business cards, a personal presentation or a one-on-one meeting, must seep deep into the subconscious mind of your prospect, provoking curiosity, desire, and a 'must-have' response.

In addition, there are certain leverage points, which may be used to advantage in your communication. For instance, we know that we will chase that which moves away from us. We will want what we cannot have. We will only place value on things that are difficult to obtain.

Your communication must include the reason for your being: your values, beliefs about the world and your place in it, your strengths, talents, and what you love. It is a combination of everything about you and your story in a way that resonates with where your prospects are, meeting them in that place where they immediately know you are the person who can help them.

This knowledge is not new. Throughout history, people have communicated and built their tribes by the way their message activates the brains of their prospective followers. In turn, they create a deep and loyal following.

For instance, the story of Robin Hood: the heroic outlaw in English folklore who has remained in the hearts of the public for centuries. Robin, a skilled archer and swordsman, became known for robbing from the rich to give to the poor. What a great strap line!

> "Don't let the noise of others' opinions drown out your own inner voice. And, most important, have the courage to follow your heart and intuition. They somehow already know what you truly want to become. Everything else is secondary."
>
> Steve Jobs, Entrepreneur, Cofounder of Apple

In Kevin Costner's 'Prince of Thieves', Robin is portrayed as an aristocrat, wrongfully deposed of his lands and made an outlaw by the unscrupulous Sherriff of Nottingham. He is assisted by his merry men, who banded together after having lost their lands and possessions in a similar way to Robin (or because they had nothing else to live for), to make good their grievances by helping those less fortunate.

The beautiful Maid Marion, being the love interest of Robin, fuels the emotions and adds to the romance. Maid Marion is portrayed as the orphaned noble woman under the protection of King John. Fiercely loyal and courageous, she ventures into Sherwood Forest with only her lady-in-waiting to accompany her, escaping the entrapment of an arranged marriage. Marion meets Robin and his merry men in the forest, and the rest, as they say, is history.

Don't we all love a great love story and happy ending?

Your Media Business Angel is a communications expert, the person to draw out your unique story so it resonates with your ideal prospects.

The copywriter or the speaking coach who will turn your expertise into written and spoken words of gold.

Exercise:

What is your story?

- How has your story led you to do what you currently do?
- How can you articulate your story into words on your website?
- How will you share your beliefs about the world and your place in it?
- Why should people follow you?

Your third business angel is able to help you in this area.

> Beliefs have the power to create and the power to destroy. Human beings have the awesome ability to take any experience of their lives and create a meaning that disempowers them or one that can literally save their lives.
>
> Tony Robbins

Step 4: Heart Business Angel
Related Chakra: Heart
Lesson: Giving and Receiving

Your heart business angel brings the lesson of giving but also of receiving. For instance, during her first year in business Amethyst Wyldfyre, 'The Empowered Messenger', explained that she gave out lots of free stuff but got nothing in return, as she had not realised how to monetise her business. She was giving, giving, and giving but not receiving.

It's a common problem, one I've personally had to deal with; and almost every entrepreneur I've ever met has to overcome this issue at some point if they are to make money.

Having a big heart for everybody else except you, by not charging enough, is not only doing a disservice to others but also it's doing a disservice to yourself, your loved ones, and your business.

There are no prizes for being in the poor house. I repeat: There are no prizes for being in the poor house.

Undercharging or giving everything for free devalues your services. It cheats your business out of the income it needs to grow. It puts a ceiling on your income and what you achieve in life.

People who receive your services at a discount or for free will not recognize the value they're receiving and therefore won't use the information in a way that gives them true value. They won't get the results expected or help you in acknowledging great results.

You have to nurture yourself to grow your business. Look at it this way; if you put a plant in a pot, it will start to grow. To look after that plant properly, you give it good compost, water, light, sunshine, and the right size of pot. It not only grows, it thrives. You have given it the nourishment, care and attention it needs, and the right environment to grow.

Eventually the plant will need a larger pot and more nourishment to continue to grow and thrive or it will become pot bound. If it doesn't receive these vital ingredients, it will become stunted and eventually die. A bonsai tree is a great example of a miniature tree, prevented from reaching its full potential. Its roots and branches are trimmed to keep it small. It survives in a tiny pot receiving the vital nourishment to keep it alive and healthy, but its not allowed to grow.

How many people do you know who live their lives like bonsai trees? How many business ideas never grow beyond the tiny pot? How many businesses die because they become pot bound and don't receive the nourishment of income to grow?

It's important to provide sufficient nourishment, care and attention, as well as creating an environment for your business to thrive. The nourishment your business needs to grow is income. Invest that income wisely.

> "We make a living by
> what we get,
> but we make a life by
> what we give."
>
> Winston Churchill

Your Heart Business Angel is the sales genius, business coach or product developer who will put together your free gifts and offers, but also package and price your services, creating a pricing strategy that works for your business. This is the business angel who will teach you how to stand your ground, to name and claim your price.

When you actively feel in your heart what you have to offer to clients is of great value, you will be safe and powerful when speaking your message.

Being financially sound puts you in a position where you can give something back to those people who struggle to afford your higher fees. By that time, you will have the time, energy, and resources to develop low-priced solutions to meet them where they're at and take them forwards.

Until you're in a position of being sufficiently strong enough to sustain your business to do that, you are still working on your inner game and nourishing your business in every way you can.

Exercise:

- What turnover do you want your business to have?
- What are the true running costs of your business?
- What salary do you want to pay yourself?
- What sales and marketing costs are you budgeting for?
- What about your coaching, mentoring, education or training course you want to go on?
- What resources do you have?
- Have you costed everything into your business?
- Add this information to a spreadsheet to get a true financial picture.

Once that first part of the exercise is completed, look at where your income is going to come from. For example: if you want to have £100,000 a year, how many clients do you need to receive that amount in income, or how many packages do you need to sell to bring in that amount?

Get coaching support from a sound business analyst to get to grips with the value of your business.

Seek out support for confidence building to get to the heart of what you are truly worth and to overcome mental blocks or self-sabotage to asking for, and receiving what you are truly worth. This is your fourth business angel.

> God wants us to
> prosper financially,
> to have plenty of money,
> to fulfill the destiny
> He has laid out for us.
>
> Joel Osteen

Step 5: Empowerment Business Angel
Related Chakra: Solar Plexus
Lesson: Awareness, Mindfulness, Power

Your empowerment business angel brings the lesson of awareness, and mindfulness, putting back your power, and raising your energy so you feel motivated and inspired. When you are in your power you will demonstrate great leadership, and take action in spite of fears or doubts while focusing on the task at hand. You will know and feel your direction with certainty.

The reality is that it can take numerous false starts in business and a number of years of feeling lost or not doing well, leading to low energy, a lack of motivation and loss of confidence, or even giving up altogether. It need not be this way if you start off by knowing who you are and how you can use your gifts and talents to contribute in a way that meets your client's needs and satisfies your inner child.

Conventional education has unfortunately not always addressed our natural resource capabilities or taught us how to tap into and use our innate abilities.

When I was a youngster, I'd often hear phrases such as 'Children should be seen, not heard', or 'Money doesn't grow on trees', and 'Respect your elders', which I did by listening to them, although I now know that much of the advice I received wasn't right for me.

This early conditioning can result in unconscious blocks, which prevent you from achieving happiness, confidence, well-being, and business success. Negative events can further compound these unconscious blocks as energy blockages in your chakras.

If you have an emotional energy blockage, your solar plexus will not be the power pack you want and need it to be. Your energy chakras all affect each other so there is a need to take a holistic approach to your personal and business issues. Common problems manifesting in business will often have hidden energetic issues. For instance:

- A lack of sales may be due to clouded or energetically conflicting personal and business goals.
- There may be poor relationships between individuals or departments. Energy work can identify and resolve these, possibly without significant changes.
- Regular bad debts may arise due to energetic limitations on personal values and the ability to receive.
- Cancelling orders may happen out of the blue, and the loss of lucrative contracts may occur due to limiting beliefs or energetic conflicts with the customer.
- Business may be an uphill struggle because it is not your true passion, and deep down, your soul is crying out to do something completely different.

Without doubt, I have blocks in my own chakras, in turn manifesting as blocks in my own business. As part of my field research for this book, I decided to experience an energy session to clear my chakras.

> "Power, after love, is the first source of happiness."
>
> Stendhal

Armed with my emotional baggage, I headed to the vibrant city of Cambridge, where just a few years ago I'd completed my master's degree in business management. I met with Jim J Doyle from the school of energy healing for a session of chakra unblocking and rebalancing.

Having completed a basic questionnaire prior to the session, we began a conversation. There's so much I can say that I eventually came out with,
"I don't know where to start".

"Start in the middle. This always works best. You can then go backwards or forwards, whichever way you feel."

Right then, I felt like Alice in Wonderland who's fallen down the rabbit hole.

When Alice meets the Cheshire cat, she says, "Would you tell me please which way I need to go from here?"

The Cat replies, "That depends a good deal on where you want to go."

"I don't much care where", says Alice, "as long as it's somewhere."

"Then it doesn't much matter which way you go", says the Cat. "You're sure to do that, if only you walk long enough."

The story of Alice in Wonderland follows Alice trying to make sense of an illogical world. Throughout the experience, she meets many challenges, odd people, and many frustrations. In the end she emerges much wiser, having learned valuable lessons as each situation occurs.

Everyone at some point faces difficult or absurd situations. If you shrug off these learning opportunities as anomalies to your perfect life, you gain nothing. But if you try to learn something from them, you will gain a lot of wisdom.

After sharing my Alice thoughts with Jim, our conversation continued with Jim directing me as we progressed. Every so often, I was told to slow down and 'breathe'. I tend to speak very quickly, words coming out of my mouth before I've engaged my brain. Slowing down can be difficult, but I realised it's something I had to do to allow Jim to assimilate and digest the information I was sharing with him.

I had a few light bulb moments too, when something popped into my mind that I'd totally forgotten. Its relevance was then obvious. It's always from my childhood.

When the conversation had run its course, we moved on to energy clearing. Lying down on a couch with a warm, woolly blanket pulled over me, I began to relax to soft musical tones playing in the background. Closing my eyes, my mind went blank.

I was aware of Jim moving around me with his hands hovering over the different parts of my body. The only time there was physical contact was when he was holding my feet, for what seemed a very long time, or briefly touching my shoulders. I felt very relaxed, almost to the point of falling asleep.

It wasn't long though before I began to experience the most amazing rush of energy into my body. It was as if all the cells in my body were waking up for the first time in years, tingling and alive.

It felt like there were parts of me that had been frozen solid and were beginning to thaw out. The experience reminded me of being in front of an open coal fire, warming up chilled hands that have been exposed to the elements for too long on a bitter cold winter's night. The heat seemed almost impossible to bear, but it was so comforting that I didn't want to say anything to disrupt the session.

At the same time, Jim was making lots of gurgling noises and deep gasping sounds, rather like belching. It reminded me of the 1999 film The Green Mile, when wrongly convicted healer John Coffey breathes out the illness or badness he's taken from someone as a cloud of flies. I'm glad in my case it's not flies.

After completing the energy session, Jim gave me feedback. Specific dates Jim mentioned do have meaning to me. These prove to be traumatic times in my life, which I can now put behind me. I felt renewed and energised at soul level.

As I left I said, "Jim, you really are my solar plexus business angel. I'd recommend anyone feeling the slightest bit of doubt, fear, or uncertainty to have a session with you to get to the root of their emotional blocks. It's like walking away with a power pack of renewed energy and self-belief inside me."

A week later I am still walking on air with renewed vigour as I embrace the necessary changes to my business I know now I must make.

As an intuitive person myself, having the ability to sense feelings and tune into energy, aligning with the soul of your business, it doesn't mean I don't need chakra rebalancing or healing myself. I do. My baggage could fill buckets.

Healing your energy chakras is very much a need of every heart-centred business owner. We tend to help others whilst denying ourselves. We all have some deep issues, and I'd highly recommend a session to re-energise and power up your system.

Your Empowerment Business Angel will strengthen your inner power, releasing emotional toxicity.

> Power can be taken, but not given.
> The process of the taking
> is empowerment in itself.
>
> Gloria Steinem

Exercise:

Go back and re-read Chapter Four on Business Chakras and Energy Connections and use the information to identify where you may have weaknesses in your chakras manifesting as problems in your business.

- Identify where you need support to re-balance your energy which in turn will power up your business.

- What actions will help you increase your personal power and self-belief?

- Do you need an energy healing session to help you feel empowered?

This is your fifth business angel.

> When they think about you, you've got to stand out in their minds like one of those characters in a novel.
>
> Candace Bushnell

Step 6: Impact Business Angel
Related Chakra: Sacral Chakra
Lesson: Impact and making a 'wow'

Your impact business angel brings the 'wow' factor into your business. This is all about how your business looks and feels. What is it that makes you stand out and get noticed?

What do you do that's different – and sexy?

How do you get your website noticed and converting to sales?

What makes people stop in their tracks and say, 'I've got to have that?'

Your impact business angel adds polish to your brand, making the little touches so you shine and illuminate your greatness.

If you offer a VIP service and are expecting VIP fees but your product or service does not stand out in a way that screams VIP, it won't attract the attention you want. Everything you do or say has to look, sound, and feel expensive in a way that attracts a VIP client.

For instance, my friend Alex is mad about Bentley cars. I would not for one minute trust myself behind the wheel of such a large and powerful car. I prefer something smaller, easier to handle, and sporty looking; whereas the Bentley oozes class and sex appeal to the wealthy rich who want the ultimate luxury classic car.

Wendy Howard

Alex doesn't own one, but it's his dream to have one in future, if only to drive for a day.

The Bentley brand is to luxury cars what Everest is to mountains, it's the ultimate achievement dream. Those who can afford the six-figure price tags of the company's vehicles are treated to the highest levels of refinement and prestige. Mostly hand-assembled in Great Britain at the manufacturer's state-of-the-art factory in Crewe, there is a fusion of old-world craftsmanship and new-world technology.

Did you know it takes 15 hours to form the Bentley leather for the steering wheel alone? If you want to learn how to make a Bentley steering wheel, it will take one full year to learn the skill. Most of the team working at Bentley come from generations of family members before them. It is indeed a privilege to work on such a beautiful car, even if you never own one.

In the beginning, W. O. Bentley started out with the idea of having a good car, a fast car, and the best in class. Making its mark in the race for more power in the 1920–1930s winning races at Le Mans in 1924; the twenty-four hour world record at Montihery. Still not satisfied, W.O. Bentley went on to launch the 6.5-litre engine in 1925, laying the foundations for the famous Speed Six racer, the innovative 4.5-litre and glorious Le Mans triumphs of 1927-1930 when the fame of Bentley's racing domination reverberated around the motoring world.

The company has a very colourful and fascinating history with much financial mess in its wake. But nothing has deterred it away from that initial idea of creating something so unique and special which, for a select few, creates a 'got to have it' moment.

Why have a VIP service?

In times of recession, people are careful what they spend their money on. To be profitable it makes sense to target people who already have the money you want for your services.

It's worth remembering that in times of hardship, the rich get richer. When property prices fall or share prices drop, that's when rich people buy. There is a sector of the market that always has the money for unique and quality services. If you don't believe me, look up the sales of Bentley during recession times.

Whether you intend being an up-market Bentley or a smaller sportier model, your business has to stand out from the rest.

The role of your Impact Business Angel is to look at your production and reproduction, creating the 'must-have' desire for your products and services, setting you apart from your competition.

This includes your branding, selecting colours, creatively presenting your business to your prospects. Your impact business angel will draw out your uniqueness, taking the words written earlier by your copy writer and transforming them into a must-have, irresistible offers through creativity, images, or videos.

Your Impact business angel brings your brand alive and sets out your VIP service to attract the VIP clients you want. This step is also about setting boundaries around how and where you work and who has access to you. Setting firm boundaries protects your personal space from those energy vampires who if allowed, would drain your resources but be unwilling to pay what you are truly worth.

Exercise:

Review your current services.

Do you offer a VIP service? If not, why not consider it? How can you make your services more appealing to attract VIP clients? What additional services can you offer that will give better value to clients?

For example: Giving someone your personal mobile number so they can call you in emergencies is much more valuable that simply giving them a telephone number to call – but you have to spell out the value to them so they recognize the value they are receiving.

It's time to stop the time wasters, and prevent those energy drains entering your space. Put up clear boundaries making it clear who it is you want to attract and who you don't. Step into the driving seat of your business and ramp up your desire and sex appeal. Need help with this step? Seek out your sixth business angel.

Step 7: Money Business Angel
Related Chakra: Base
Lesson: Financial Acumen, Investing, Healthy Relationship to Money

Your money business angel brings the lesson of financial acumen, investing wisely and also strengthens your relationship to money. When your business is up and running, your ideas are formulated into products and services, and there is money coming into your business, then your money flow is positively activated.

Don't become complacent at this time. Take care and reinvest income into your business so that it grows.

Understanding numbers is not something that comes naturally to many people, especially with so many other areas of the business to concentrate on. Numbers and financial forecasting can be very confusing, which is why many people sweep the issue under the carpet. The attitude is "If I can't see it, it doesn't exist."

This is not true. You are hiding your head in the sand. At some point you will have to deal with the monetary issues which will undoubtedly arise.

Are you someone who believes in your accountant taking care of all your monetary issues? Your accountant puts together your end-of-year profit and loss and balance sheet to complete your tax return. The information they need to do this has to come from you so it makes sense to keep good records.

The problem with relying on your accountant solely in this way is that you are viewing historical data. You have a snapshot in time. This is good information to review what you did or didn't do. But as an entrepreneur, you need to be on top of your numbers at all times, learning how to forecast and play with numbers effectively, making the best profits and decisions for your business.

Leading accountant-turned-entrepreneur and author of the book Profit Rocket, Kelly Clifford says, "Playing with numbers can be fun." Kelly makes understanding your numbers simple and interesting.

Not making sufficient money to invest in the training you need or not finding the time to seek out the people who will teach you the skills to grow your business and to get the support you need will hold you back.

You can take immediate action by following these steps:

Step 1: Take Responsibility

Accept where you currently are, whatever the situation is. You are in this situation because of your own actions. It is not because of the economy, people not having money to invest in your products and services, or any other excuse you care to give.

The reality is you are where you are because of the choices you have made, the decisions you have taken, and the actions or inactions you have made so far. There is no right or wrong. It's just as it is.

Acknowledge personal responsibility and commit to regain your power.

Step 2: Check out your Attitude

The connection between attitude and success is undeniable. Changing attitude can be one of the most difficult things to do.

Motivational teacher John Maxwell, in his book The Difference Maker, says, "One of the things motivational speakers say a lot, which I disagree with, is that attitude is everything. If you can believe it, you can achieve it, they say. What you set your mind to can become yours. I don't think it works that way. I know a lot of good people who have a wonderful attitude who haven't reached their dreams yet."

John explains that your attitude cannot substitute for competence, experience, or changing the facts. Your attitude cannot substitute for personal growth. Nor will your attitude stay good automatically.

For instance, I will never be a brain surgeon because I'm not competent or experienced enough in medical training to be one. Nor will I ever be an opera singer, for as much as I love opera I do not have an operatic voice or the aptitude to be an opera singer. My singing voice is more like a cat wailing. That's a fact. Changing my attitude will not change that fact.

What your attitude can do is make a difference in your approach to life. If you give something your best shot and go in with a great attitude, chances are you will come away with the best outcome.

Your attitude makes a difference in your relationships with people. Having your own views and perspective is one thing, but viewing it from someone else's perspective will give you greater insight and understanding.

Your attitude makes a difference in how you face challenges. It's not that successful people have fewer problems than unsuccessful people. They just have a different mindset.

Sir Winston Churchill once said,

> "A pessimist sees the difficulty in every opportunity; an optimist sees the opportunity in every difficulty."

Check out your attitude and if it is not serving you, change it.

Step 3: Make a Decision

Choose today to make a decision to do things differently from now on. Stop doing things that don't matter, which drain your energy and resources. Do the things that do matter, and it will make a huge difference. Face up to the challenges of growing your business profitably by finding the help, support, and resources you need to grow.

I recall meeting Stephen Pierce at a conference in Wembley Stadium some time ago. Stephen is a shining example of what can happen when you take responsibility for where you are at the present time, change your attitude, and make a decision to do things differently from now on.

Stephen has the most amazing stage presence, and I hung onto every word he shared. He stood in the centre of this huge stage, silent to begin with, anticipation in the air, and not a peep of sound from the thousands of people in the audience, totally spellbound, as we waited for him to begin.

> *"Today is the last day of the brokest year of the rest of your life. Repeat after me."*

And the thousands of voices repeating those words rang out across Wembley Stadium, not once, not twice, but three times. I've never forgotten them, in part, because of Stephen's great presence, certainty, and honesty.

Stephen's life was on a downward spiral almost from the moment of his birth. Drugs, alcohol, homelessness, debt, and finally a bullet in his leg, which remains to this day because he didn't have the insurance cover for the surgery to remove it. He could very well have ended up dead. Instead, Stephen says, "Your outcome is based on what you are willing to overcome."

Exercise:

Go to the resources page on the website www.7businessangels.com and you will find links to help you discover your money type and begin to explore your relationship with money.

Your Money Business Angel is the numbers wizard with the financial acumen to secure the future of your business and legacy. In doing so, you will begin to explore the relationship you have with money and where you may need to change the values driving that relationship. This is your seventh business angel.

By adding the relevant expertise and input of all seven business angels into your business angel plan, and taking the action required at each step you will build your business on solid foundations. You may apply this seven step process to launch your business as a whole, or for individual products or services, promote your book and make a positive impact with your valuable contribution.

Your Seven Business Angel Steps

BUSINESS ANGEL	BUSINESS ACTION	CHAKRA	RELATED EMOTION	STATE	SPIRITUAL LESSON	COLOUR	GEMSTONE
Concept	Idea Formation.	Crown	Attachment, devotion, trust, loss of meaning or identity, selflessness, values, ethics	The right to know	Intuitive knowing, living in the NOW	Violet/White	Amber, Diamond Star Tulip
Clarity	Taking your idea forward, planning what's next and getting clear on unique path, product and service. Setting firm goals and action plan.	Third Eye/Intuitive	Illusion, fear of truth, evaluation, concept of reality, emotional intelligence	The right to see	Understanding, reality check, detachment, open mind	Indigo	Purple Flourite, Sugilite, Lapis
Media	Words, writing copy, speaking, communicating with your target audience.	Throat	Personal expression, creativity, faith, decision making, addiction, lies, lack of connection, confusion	The right to speak and hear the truth	Confession, faith, truthfulness over deceit	Sky Blue	Chrysocolla, Lapis Blue Opal
Heart	Pricing strategy, charging enough to make profits.	Heart	Love, compassion, generosity, hurt, rejection, sorrow, resentment, hate, envy, jealousy	The right to love and be loved	Forgiveness, trust, unconditional love, letting go, compassion	Green	Malachite Emerald Rose Quartz
Empowerment	Self Belief, increasing self esteem, gaining confidence, re-balancing self	Solar Plexus	Self-esteem, fear of rejection, self image, fears, indecisiveness, fear of secrets being found out	The right to feel	Acceptance of oneself in the life stream, self love	Yellow	Jasper Golden Topaz Yellow Tourmaline
Impact	Effect and impact on others, client attraction.	Sacral Chakra	Power, guilt, blame, control, morality	Emotional flow	Creativity, manifestation, learning to let go	Orange	Garnet Moonstone Orange Tourmaline
Money	Money is now flowing into your business. Money management and financial planning.	Base	Fear, blind panic, survival, security, social order, family	The right to be here	Material world lessons	Red	Hematite Black Tourmaline, Onyx

Chapter Seven:

Illuminate Your Business Heart
Lizzie's Story

We live in an incredibly beautiful world within an amazing and forever - expanding universe. As quickly as our scientists make new discoveries, growing our body of knowledge, giving further insight into the phenomenal wonder of our world today, the questions become deeper and the answers seemingly more complex and further out of reach.

Business today is certainly more complex than it was before we had the internet, regardless of it having opened up the world marketplace to anyone who wants it. Non-the-less, problems in finding clients and having a financially sound business remain difficult for many heart-centered businesses.

Recently, I had the privilege to work with Lizzie, a coach and healing practitioner. Lizzie has years of experience working with clients, helping them overcome deep trauma. Her clients are often ostracised on the edge of society and life when they arrive at her door. She is often their last hope for coming to terms with deeply emotional and mentally disturbing issues, which at times have halted or stunted their lives.

Meeting Lizzie, I was in no doubt that she possessed a unique skill and ability to reach deep into the chasms of the person's psyche, rooting out the trauma, healing the hurt, and enabling the person to move forward. Lizzie explained that sometimes her clients only needed one or two sessions before the transformation took place, leaving the client feeling completely whole again.

Unfortunately, Lizzie's invaluable work gave her a problem. After a particularly difficult session with a client, she would feel anything but whole herself. Instead she would feel vulnerable and tired. Lizzie explained that she regularly needed time out from her business to recover her energy. When things were really bad, Lizzie was unable to function, and bed rest was essential to aid recovery.

Then we discussed the issue of money. Lizzie's clients could not always afford to pay her fees, and sometimes when she was paid, her fees were limited by the charity sponsoring the client. This put a ceiling on her earning potential.

Immediately I sensed a disconnection between Lizzie's work, business aspirations, and personal well-being. I sat down with Lizzie and we had a thorough intuitive business destiny reading to assess the strengths and weaknesses in Lizzie's business but also to explore the deeper sub-conscious issues Lizzie held which were manifesting as problems and negativity in her business.

I worked through each step with Lizzie as follows:

i. Business Destiny Reading

This is the starting point for all my business clients and usually takes between sixty and ninety minutes. During this time as I did with Lizzie, I take the client through a series of conversational questions. I use intuition to guide me on how this conversation goes and I will instinctively feel where the issues or blocks are within the person, which are manifesting as issues or problems in their business. I will also use business acumen to see what stage of growth the business is at in line with what the person wants to achieve. I can then decide which tools or techniques will work with the individual person and business.

In Lizzie's case she had a belief that she had to work hard to prove she was worthy. Her belief kept Lizzie busy to the point of exhaustion whereby her body said 'enough' and it responded by making her ill so she had to take time out. We explored the root cause of this belief and the deeper issues, which were held at a sub-conscious level. Once we had identified where these beliefs were by using muscle testing and then Theta healing techniques we could change these beliefs to more positive and supportive beliefs.

For instance, Lizzie held a belief that the only way to earn money was by working hard, and in Lizzie's case this interpreted as having to keep herself busy. Being ill, and taking time out caused further internal wrangling because Lizzie believed that she was then letting her clients down because she wasn't available to help them and therefore felt she must be lazy. This made her feel guilty and in her own words 'how useless she really was' which of course fueled her belief that she wasn't worthy of receiving money – so she didn't.

An intuitive business destiny reading goes much deeper than the problems manifesting in the business, it will uncover the subconscious thoughts manifesting those problems and driving the disruptive or destructive behaviour.

When we know what the beliefs are we can then explore the deeper issues of where those beliefs have developed and what level. In Lizzie's case, they were from the work ethic instilled in her as a child, but went back a number of generations in her family. Beliefs may lie on up to four different levels; the Core Belief level, the History level, the Genetic level and the Soul level. By identifying the level and bottom belief we can accept to change it.

It is sometimes the case whereby someone is drawn towards the work they do well with clients, because they are gifted in that area, and yet fail to take their own medicine. They are so close to their work and able to gain incredible results with clients but unable to manifest the necessary change within themselves – because they can't see past the block or know the cause of it.

ii. Business Alignment

The business alignment process is the next step. With Lizzie we looked at the potential of the business and the possible directions she could grow her client base to increase her income.

It's important to find the heart-centre of the business, as it's the platform for all future growth and income as well as bringing fulfillment to the person whose business it is. This part is the first step of the business angel plan.

Lizzie had definitely found her niche and she wanted to continue with her work and at the same time remain open to helping some clients who could not afford to pay her fees. To allow her to do that we had to create a plan which sustained regular income into her business, and this would allow her to give back some of that income and time to those clients who could not afford to pay. We also had to set up a series of work and personal boundaries for Lizzie to prevent her expanding her energy to the point of exhaustion. During this creative session we looked at the most viable options for the business inline with the Lizzie's aspirations. This can be a challenging session and may conflict with money beliefs.

iii. Business Angel Plan

The third part of the process is to put together the business angel plan. This included all seven achievable steps over an agreed period of time. As part of this plan I identified the profile of the business angels Lizzie needed to meet as she progressed with her plan. We set out the actions into an achievable timeline making it easy for Lizzie to follow and be accountable.

Working with Lizzie in this way we began creating a clear route to grow her business that was in line with her desired goals and personal values. This enabled greater vision and clarity. Developing packages, which still allowed her to help some clients who couldn't afford to pay full professional fees, fulfilled Lizzie's desire to give something back.

Critical elements of Lizzie's on-going plan included:

- Business Destiny Reading to fully assess the current situation and identify weaknesses manifesting as business problems. Using intuition, questioning, muscle testing and Theta healing techniques to get to the bottom belief and root cause of the issues. Becoming aware of reasons for problems or blocks is empowering. Lizzie's plan included identifying the potential for maximising income and steps to do that. We also identified any future problems and how to avoid or deal with as they arise.

- Business Alignment strategies brought together personal values to grow the business from the heart centre. For Lizzie, we created a number of packages with differing price levels and a concessionary payment scheme for those in need of this service.

- Putting in place prevention techniques to help Lizzie recognise energy drains which triggers her exhaustion, thus lowering the need to take time out from her business.

- Developing firm boundaries for both personal and business life, including how to deal with challenges conflicting with these boundaries.

- Further exploring the relationship with work ethos and money challenges to uncover the psychological roots manifesting as money blocks and strategies on how to overcome these.

- Learning how to activate positivity to attract money in, putting into practice the universal law of giving and receiving.

- Business Angel Plan for long-term growth, increased expertise, and building a support network of business angels for each of the seven key business-building steps.

It's a dilemma for many heart-centred entrepreneurs not just Lizzie, who tend to be giving by nature and super sensitive to the needs of others that on a personal level they feel drained of energy. They are 'tuned in' to help people, but ingrained in their psyche is the inability to ask for just financial rewards in exchange for their services, or the tendency to seek the help they badly need themselves.

As an entrepreneur, your business is a direct reflection of what is already set inside of you. Healers and practitioners will often heal others but are unable to make money because there is a need to heal something within themselves.

Cyndi Dale, internationally respected author and spiritual scholar, calls this 'The Healer's Syndrome', where you have a heart as big as the world, but 'the world' doesn't include you. Then you become burdened with the problems you are fixing. You give without receiving anything in return.

The truth is that your business will only ever grow to be as big as you do.

Your business offers you the most amazing opportunity for personal growth and an opportunity to view what other aspects are not working in all areas of your life. In the words of T. Harv Eker, "How you do anything, is how you do everything" and as a heart-centred entrepreneur how you live your life and how you respond to people or situations is very much how you will run your business and deal with business issues.

The paradox is that those with the biggest hearts nurture a need to help and heal others on a deep soul level. It is a calling.

Asking for money and deserving payment in return can feel uncomfortable, but it is essential to learn how to do this well and recognise the true value of your services.

Your monetary income is the 'fuel' to growing your business and helping more people. When you nurture your business from a soul level, you will feel worthier, value your services on a deeper level, and your business will bring in the income you want. In addition you will find yourself in a much better position to reach and help more people than you ever thought possible. Money is the exchange mechanism you use to do your work more efficiently and effectively. You can't do your work unless you receive sufficient income in return for your services.

My work with clients involves working on the individual, the emotional, the mental, and the spiritual levels. Building your business this way enables you to illuminate your services from the heart centre, the soul of your business. They do not teach this in business school.

Money is not the issue. It never is. It is your relationship with money, which creates doubt uncertainty and fear. When you change your relationship with money and recognize the value within yourself, you will become a magnet for positivity. Remember: You are your number one most valuable asset!

The outcome for Lizzie was extremely positive. The seven step plan we'd developed had very shortly tripled her earning potential, and as Lizzie's confidence grew, she saw an increasing flow of private fee-paying clients. The boundaries we'd put in place prevented her from running her energy too low. Instead, she was taking time out from her business and it was having a positive effect on her well-being and her relationship with her partner and family. She had begun to enjoy life again, which had sadly been forgotten in the rush to build her business.

In addition, Lizzie challenged the low income she'd been receiving for clients passed to her via charities and had stipulated a higher fee – which to her disbelief they were happy to accept. As with universal law – ask and it will be given. If you do not ask you will never know. Rock on Lizzie!

> Your self-worth has nothing to do with your craft or calling, and everything to do with how you treat yourself.
>
> Kris Carr

Part Two

Evolution, Your Quirky Brain And Adding Your Contribution

Everyone in
this world is
somehow connected.
So why not
just be nice
to everybody.

Richard Simmons

Chapter Eight

The New Feminine Business Economy In Our Powerful Digital Communications Age

We're privileged to be living in the most amazing digital communications age, where you can reach anyone on our immense planet at any time within a few seconds.

Like billions of others, you and I are accustomed to using the Internet on a daily basis. Look around and you will see the majority of people connected by an invisible umbilical cord to a smart phone or other device, oblivious to what is happening in the world around them.

Joining social media networks to market your business is the norm. At the very least, you are likely to be on LinkedIn, YouTube, Facebook, Twitter and Google+. The speed of your communication is a mere nanosecond - light years away from that of your ancestors.

Growing up in the small town in Alnwick, Northumberland, my grandfather built a legacy out of his small grocery business. Like many inspirational people of his generation, he employed the popular model of the corner shop supplying the townsfolk with everything they needed, right on their doorstep. In later years, he added a butcher's shop and hairdressing salon.

Fast forward a generation or so, grandfather long gone, I returned to find a new housing estate where my grandfather's shop had once stood. The butcher's shop and hairdressing salon were both gone too. I don't think my grandfather could ever have envisioned the future of his little empire.

Yet, I still feel my grandfather's entrepreneurial spirit within, the true legacy. Every generation leaves an imprint affecting the people in its wake.

As a mother of three daughters, and now a grandmother too, I find this a very different world than the one I grew up in. Do you ever stop to wonder what the legacy of this digital communications age is likely to be for generations to come?

Recently, rather disturbingly, a four-year-old girl became Britain's youngest iPad addict after displaying compulsive behaviour with the device. Thousands of children like her are addicted to games and in need of treatment for withdrawal symptoms. Doctors have noted children becoming inconsolable when separated from their phones or tablets (Daily Mail, April 23rd 2013).

Childcare author Tanith Carey says, "iPads and smartphones have become the new dummies for babies and toddlers." While many parents confiscate their child's device as a punishment, some admit this approach has sparked a tantrum, branded as the iPaddy.

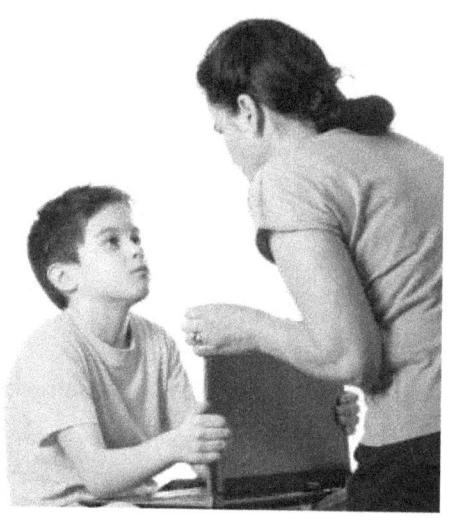

Of course, tech-savvy entrepreneurs are keen to jump on the latest trends by creating inventions to fulfill the desires of our digital age youngsters.

For instance, we now have the iPotty for toddlers. It's described as a comfortable and child-friendly potty with activity stand, so that your child need never be separated from his or her apps, even during toilet training.

Without doubt, the digital age we are in and how it will affect our lives for generations to come has many similarities to the 1999 film The Matrix, which depicts a dystopian future in which reality as perceived by most humans is actually a simulated reality called 'the Matrix'.

The Matrix was created by sentient machines to subdue the human population, while the heat of their bodies and electrical brain activity are used as an energy source. Computer programmer 'Neo' learns the truth and is drawn into a rebellion against the machines, involving other people who have been freed from their 'dream world'.

How we live our lives today is causing us to enter into a digitally enhanced dream world, while at the same time battling internally to escape from the Matrix we've created.

Global change has affected everyone to some extent in recent years. We witness the rise and fall of giant corporations as one by one they go to the wall. who'd ever have imagined the closing of once up on a time high street favourite Woolworths? Thousands of people have lost their financial future to the collapse of the banking system. Some local councils in the UK were badly burned by this collapse having been ill advised to place their money in banks in Iceland for a higher interest return, not envisaging the collapse of the banking system or the ensuing fallout. Emerging global markets in China, India, Brazil, and other parts of the world are seeing a whole shift of balance and power.

Evolutionary changes are happening on a global scale, but far removed from the naysayers and negative messages the media gives out, this is the golden digital age of opportunity. I believe we have entered the age of prosperity our ancestors prophesised about.

This global shift evokes a change towards increased personal responsibility and, giving back our individual power. With unlimited evolutionary growth we can peek through the veils of time, gaining access to the diamonds laid down by the great masters who have gone before carving the path for us.

There is lightness in the new feminine economy bringing a fresh approach of collaboration without the barriers of previous generations. The feminine economy is making a radical shift from the love of power to the power of love. We are moving away from the feelings of separation, shifting from a world of dualistic thinking to the consciousness of Oneness.

> Keep love in your heart.
> A life without
> it is like a
> sunless garden
> when the flowers
> are dead.
>
> Oscar Wilde

Embracing the new feminine business economy brings an acceptance of the powerful influence of universal energy in business and the promise of freedom and prosperity.

In doing so, you have to learn new ways of doing and being. You have to rediscover who you are and who you were meant to be. You have to understand that as soon as you grasp one concept, the rules will have already changed.

But are we so switched on digitally that we are at risk of switching off to the massive universal power and feminine energy sweeping through our time?

If you remain locked into a dream world of believing there is never enough, you will be immune to the universal clues when they are given to you. You will be blind to the actions you need to take. You will be unlikely to meet and connect with the business angels who will help secure your legacy.

Connecting and changing paths is something you must do if you are to add your contribution to the world, leaving a positive imprint for generations to come.

In the new feminine economy it is every bit as important to switch off and tune into the universal lightness as it is to be able to switch on and benefit from the powerful digital communications age.

Our prime purpose
in this life
is to help others.
And if you
can't help them,
at least
don't hurt them.

Dalai Lama

Chapter Nine

Myths, Truths, And Sand
Is Money Really Your Biggest Hurdle?

Why are you here? What is your purpose? What is your mission? How often do you ask yourself these questions? When you do, are you left searching for the answers?

At times, it may seem you are but a single grain of sand on the great beaches of time. When your life is done, the waves of life's ocean will wash you away, and your existence will fade into the centuries of history. That's life.

All that matters is now: the impact you make in the world and your contribution to our universe. You may ask, "What use am I if I'm compared to a tiny grain of sand?" Let me tell you that you and your work matter a great deal.

There are few things in the world as simple as a grain of sand, and perhaps none more complex than a computer chip. Yet, do you know the simple element silicon in sand is the starting point for making the integrated circuits that power everything from supercomputers to cell phones and microwave ovens?

Sand: they're powerful tiny grains on the beaches of time. Turning sand into tiny devices with millions of components is an extraordinary feat of science and engineering that would have seemed impossible just a few decades ago. Isn't that amazing?

Yet, as a human being, very much like the grain of sand, if you are given the right environment, the right conditions, and the right people around you, you will no longer be ordinary - you will become extraordinary. It's a fact of nature. A miraculous transformation will occur.

You may be facing difficulties right now or be unsure of your next steps. You may have hit an income plateau, and you may not be sure how to overcome it. You may be attracting insufficient or unqualified leads, wasting too much time on the unimportant things that don't matter.

Let me help you by exploding some of the common myths you may already have fallen prey to. I know because I've tripped up myself in the past and I want to share these so you can avoid them.

> Your success and happiness lies in you.
> Resolve to keep happy, and your joy and you shall form an invincible host against difficulties.
>
> Helen Keller

Myths and Truths

Myth One:
It's all about the numbers. You must play the numbers game, building a huge following to be successful.

Truth:
Nothing is further from the truth. What you need is proper targeting, positioning, and presentation strategies. A small list that has been generated properly will give you a higher response and conversion rate every time.

Myth Two:
You have to present your logical arguments, facts and figures, and features and benefits to grab your prospect's attention.

Truth:
Your logical arguments do not immediately register with your prospect's brain. There is a process you have to go through first to ensure your message is picked up by your prospect and that it gets the response you want.

Myth Three:
You have to be good at sales, overcoming objections and closing the deal. You must trap people with time-limited offers or value-added incentives to get them to sign on the dotted line.

Truth:
These are manipulations. This starts the relationship off in the wrong way. Unfortunately, sales has earned a bad reputation due to some people having brought what is a great service into a not-so-good practice. Good salesmanship is about service, not trapping or manipulating people by shoe-horning them into something that isn't a good fit for them.

When you're disconnected, low on energy and resources, what appears to be a quick and easy solution can prove to be an expensive distraction or mistake.

The following case studies will shed light on this:

Case Study One

Meeting June, I recognised her as a classic example of someone getting in her own way. Very talented and creative, June designs and makes beautiful pieces of bespoke furniture. Each piece is carefully crafted into a beautiful, unique work of art, designed to the exact desires and expectations of her clients. June spends many hours on her work, often burning the midnight oil to deliver a high-quality product for her delighted clients.

June loves her work but could not sell or represent her business well. The very thought of standing up in front of a group of people and speaking or giving a presentation made her feel ill. June would tremble, physically shaking from head to foot. June felt she was letting everyone down, including herself, and she'd rather not face that situation at all.

When terrified of success, failing often seems the easier option. The result was that June did not attract lucrative clients. She was surviving by taking on low-paid, unrewarding work which, when she worked it out, often didn't pay minimum wage. June was tired, barely paying her rent and had not had a holiday for almost six years.

June explained she'd tried many traditional methods of marketing: leaflets, flyers, advertising, asking friends for referrals, and dabbling on social media. Almost in tears, June admitted I was her last resort. But, like many struggling entrepreneurs, she didn't believe she would be able to afford my services.

One of the biggest hurdles to overcome is the money issue. How can you get what you know you need and want when you do not have the money to invest? June saw this as her biggest dilemma.

I did not. All I asked June to do initially was to make a commitment to work with me. That's all. June agreed.

Truth is, it does not take long to turn a business around if, like June, you have a great product or service. The problem is that many people see the gap between where they are now to where they want to be as being too wide. When you do this, you fall into the hole you've created and it's impossible to see other possibilities exist. When you're in that mindset of not enough it keeps you where you are. It puts a stopper in the money flow, preventing it from reaching you.

The solution is to concentrate only on the next step, the one that is directly in front of you. When you reach that step, you then move towards the following step. Keep moving forward one step at a time. That's all you need to do. Keep your focus on the next step. This way it's not so daunting. Progress becomes very achievable.

June and I began working together by initially having a business reading. This session enabled us to go deeply into all areas of the business to assess what is working and what isn't, as well as to assess where the real problems were manifesting from. We then assessed the current money situation and income potential for June's business.

June's self-belief was low giving her communication problems when speaking. June was not in her power and lacking confidence. It's important to point out that problems manifesting in the business tend to be inter-linked as nothing is ever in isolation. This is why a holistic approach is necessary.

Getting to the real issues preventing success such as underlying values and personal subconscious beliefs is critical. Without this assessment and putting steps into place to prevent self-sabotage, you will not feel strengthened sufficiently to support business success. This is why a Business Angel plan works well, because as you work through each step and engage with others who can fix your problems or assist you in that area, you are naturally strengthening every level of yourself and developing the business skills by taking the actions recommended.

A business is similar to the analogy of building a house. Most of the initial work goes into the planning, design, and laying firm foundations to support the building and bringing in experts such as architects, plumbers, carpenters, electricians and brick layers for each building phase. Erecting the house takes much less time than the initial design, planning, and laying of foundations. It is the same with your business. It needs careful planning and laying of firm foundations for stability to grow, and bringing in experts: your business angels at each phase of growth.

When your mind opens up to the amazing opportunities and possibilities for business success your brain will start to work towards achieving rather than sabotaging, and results will follow. June was no exception.

Following our agreed seven-step business angel plan, it didn't take long for June to begin to break through. Calling me early one morning, she excitedly blurted out that she'd just received a commission from a large solicitor's firm in London asking for a number of bespoke pieces of furniture.

Best of all, they were willing to pay a large fee upfront from their refurbishment budget, which equated to more than her last two years' income!

How's that for a great return on investment?

Initially June believed that to be successful in business, she needed to make presentations to large groups of people. She battled daily with her reluctance to stand up and sell. Her fear, so deeply engrained, became a paralysing phobia.

After explaining to June that talks and presentations to large groups of people are simply tactics, they're not strategy, June relaxed. With the right strategy in place and aligning the tactics to her natural and preferred way of communicating, it became a recipe for success. June had mastered her unique recipe. What a relief it was to her that she did not need to stand up in front of large groups to be successful!

June is now following a seven step business angel plan, which strengthens her on a deep personal level too, increasing her confidence and self-belief. In turn this strength is reflected into her business success.

> Courage is never to let your actions be influenced by your fears.
>
> Arthur Koestler

Case Study Two

Meeting Roger, an NLP practitioner and coach, his warm smile and firm handshake were welcoming.

Roger shared his personal story: "Redundancy finally gave me the opportunity to start my own business. I thought, 'Freedom at last. No longer will I be a slave working long hours or bound and stifled by corporate bureaucracy.' I immediately set about enhancing my already good people skills by training in NLP techniques and gaining a master coaching certificate."

"Then I set about writing a formal business and marketing plan, which I believe is essential. From there, I had my logo, business cards, website, and branding designed and put in place. But where are the clients willing to pay my fees? It feels like I'm pulling teeth."

Admirably, Roger belonged to a number of local networking groups and was building a presence on social media, following the advice of his mentor. Roger confided his frustration compounded by the need to support his wife and growing family.

Roger continued, "I can see the lack of belief in their eyes when I return home from yet another meeting with a couple of leads and a handful of business cards. My money is running out, and I must generate an income soon, or it's back to finding a job. My heart sinks at that thought because I really believe I can do this. I love the world of coaching and being able to transform lives."

Thanking Roger for being honest with me, I reassured him he wasn't doing anything wrong. Much of what he'd done so far was heading in the right direction.

I explained that it's a very noisy place in the entrepreneurial world, and coaching is a crowded field. It's not enough to build your business based on your passion in the hope they will come. They won't.

Initially to assess where Roger was at, I began by asking him: "Roger, take me through your business in your own words from beginning to end. Tell me about your products and services and what you do for clients. How do you offer your services to them? In what way do you help them? What results can they expect when working with you?"

Roger began by rattling off a long list of the services he offered. It sounded like a well-stocked gift shop with so many choices, I felt confused. Its overwhelming for prospective clients when you offer too many options. Roger did not offer a solution to his prospective clients specific problems, therefore they went instead to the person offering exactly what they wanted to alleviate their problem.

Offering multiple choices was diluting Roger's focus in communications too, as he was giving out mixed messages. When Roger spoke about his business, he darted from one place to another.

I offered, "Roger, imagine you're out walking on a dark winter's night and carrying a torch to light your way. The torch beam is focused on the road ahead, so everything else is in darkness. If you keep the beam focused on the road ahead, you will eventually get to your destination.

But, if your torch beam deviates elsewhere, this is where your focus will go. In other words, if you do not have one clear path, or one clear message, and keep deviating or wandering down another route altogether, then this is where your focus will go. The more paths you have to focus on, the more difficult it is to reach a destination, if you ever do."

By this time Roger sat up straight and more alert, thoughtfully nodding his head in agreement.

I continued in a slightly different vein, "Roger, do you ever go fishing?"

"Yes, strangely enough it was a hobby of mine I enjoyed when much younger," he said. "I'd like to find the time to do it again. It's very therapeutic and so relaxing."

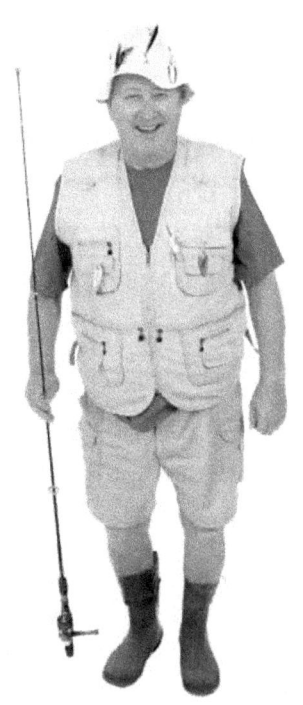

"Well, think about your business as if you're on a fishing trip," I said, "To fish properly, you need the right equipment, the right environment and the right bait for the job. To keep it simple, a pool full of fish, a rod and a line to catch fish with, and some bait to tempt the fish to bite."

"But if you are fishing for salmon and the pool you're fishing in is full of eels, you won't catch any salmon. Similarly, if you're fishing in a pool full of salmon but the bait you have is for eels, the salmon will not bite. Again, you will not catch any fish." Roger nodded his head in agreement. I continued, "Your business works in a similar way. You need to place your hook in the right environment, with the correct bait your people are hungry for.

They will snap right at it. When it works, you can set out more fishing lines in more pools with the right bait for what is in those pools and repeat the process. Make sense?"

With this agreed, we set about finding the right hook, preparing the bait, and seeking out the right pool for Roger's business. We identified one key central core product to Roger's business. Then working through each step of the business angel plan we identified the progress steps Roger would need to have in place and the people who could help him

Three months later, Roger's business is steadily growing as he's crafting out his niche. He's working fewer hours, concentrating his time on the most beneficial activities for business growth. Best of all, Roger has found a new hobby - not fishing, but golf, something he'd always promised himself he would do one day.

I feel privileged to work with people like June and Roger, who both want to make a difference and personal contribution through their own business ideas.

Taking heart-centred entrepreneurs through an initial Business Destiny Reading to identify core beliefs and blocks and then setting out a creative Seven Step Business Angel Plan and sourcing the resources and people I term your Business Angels to enable you to grow and increase income is a pleasure.

Connecting with your business angels does not tend to happen in the conventional way. You'll learn why this is in the next chapter when we focus on the quirky workings of the brain.

Your mind is a magnet.
You don't attract
what you need
or what you want;
you attract who you are.

Carlos Santana

Chapter Ten

Your Quirky Brain
Power Up Your Thoughts

A friend of mine, Stephen, has a saying when things go wrong in his life, "Why do I always end up with the rough end of the pineapple, while others get to sip on a pina colada?"

I know exactly what he means. If anyone can attract the pointy ends of the pineapple - life's crap and chaos - Stephen can. If there's a water-filled hole in the sidewalk, he won't see it and will step right in, soaking his boots and drenching the bottoms of his neatly pressed jeans. If a bird is flying overhead and decides to drop a poop, it's guaranteed it will land on his head rather than on the person walking next to him.

The question is, do we all subconsciously invite certain incidents to happen? If so, how? And does your brain govern the level of success you will achieve in life and in business? And how does your communication influence whether a prospect receives your sales message and acts positively, or not at all?

One thing is for sure, the complex workings of the brain affect each and every one of us, including seemingly unconnected events that just 'seem to happen'. In this chapter, you will find information that has the power to transform your life and business.

At my deepest depths of business despair - and believe me, there have been more despairing moments than I care to remember on my entrepreneurial journey which I now see as learning opportunities, I recall my then-coach saying: "You have to have the breakdown before you get the breakthrough" and, "It's always darkest before the dawn." How true those few words are. I came to realise that if things had to change, then it was down to me to make those changes. I set out to find the missing link.

The secret was closer to home than I'd ever imagined. You see, it wasn't to do with anyone else. It was all to do with me. Or rather, my quirky brain.

To keep it simple, your brain is a magnificent filtering system. Imagine it like this. In your home you have electricity, which powers your lights, your fridge, freezer, your computers, and anything else electrical. Everything is connected and fuelled by this invisible power source. Your home will also have a fuse box. When it is overloaded with this invisible power, it triggers out. It will not work again until you fix it by replacing the blown fuse or eliminating the power overload in the system that caused it to trigger out.

Your brain is wired and works in a similar way. Like having a fuse box, your brain will trigger out when it is overloaded with too much information. To prevent this overload, it has a filtering system that limits the information, keeping it to a manageable level so that you don't blow a fuse. Your brain does this to keep you safe.

Depending on how your brain is set to filter information, it will prevent you from receiving messages or seeing opportunities that may be beneficial to your success. This important information is fused out, and you don't even know it is happening. Your brain is set to keep you safe, not to make you successful.

Your brain's programming and re-tuning for success.

To understand the workings of your brain in more detail, studies in the 1950s showed that the smallest number of pieces of information your mind receives on a daily basis is two million per second.

You can't process all of this information consciously. This is why your brain must have a filtering system in place.

What does come through to your conscious awareness is only what you have programmed your mind to offer. The rest is filtered out in a way that is sometimes described as the 'red car syndrome.'

In other words, you don't notice red cars on the road until you buy one. Then you become aware of red cars on the road, which are similar models to yours. Your brain filters out those cars for you, bringing them into your conscious mind. This is an example of the most basic filtering system your mind uses daily. You have to re-tune your brain to filter in the success you want.

Why your communications in business succeed or fail.

What I'm about to share with you next is based on research compiled by Dorina Lanza, a medical physicist, business strategy consultant, mergers and acquisitions vice president, and university professor in Boston.

Dorina explains that in 1952, Paul Maclean, a neuroscientist, hypothesised that the human brain is really made up of three brains, each evolving consecutively:

Wendy Howard

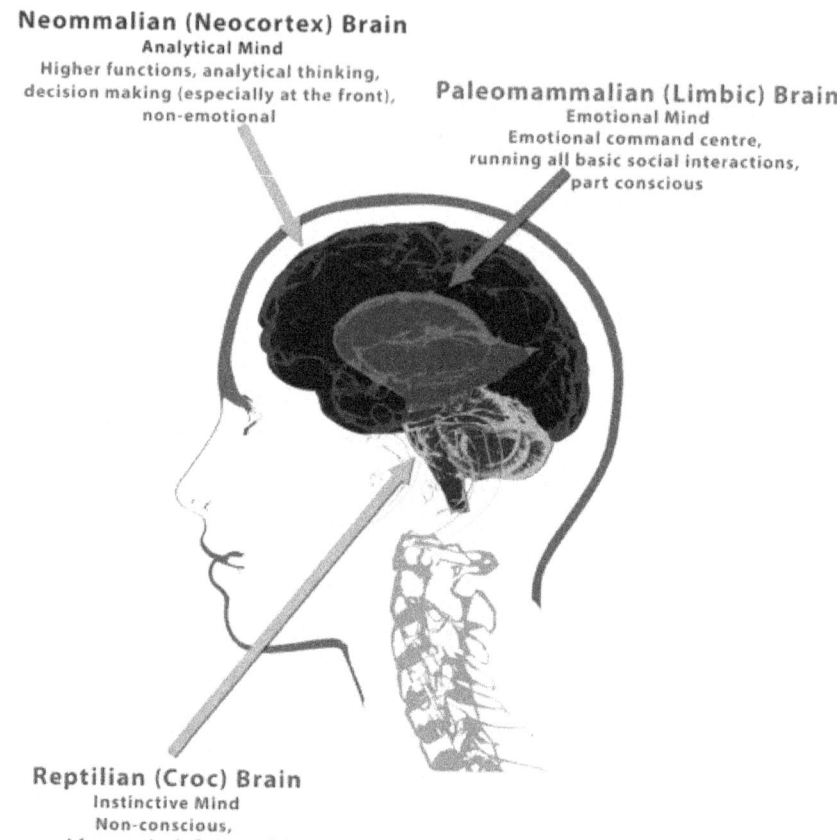

Brain One:

The reptilian (croc brain) first developed hundreds of millions of years back.

Brain Two:

The paleomammalian (limbic system).

Brain Three:

The neomammalian (neocortex).

Your earliest developed brain, the reptilian or 'croc' brain, deals with human survival and keeping your body functioning. It is the part of the brain that kept your ancestors safe by warning them about predators and urging them to run away from danger back in the days before we were civilized as we are today. The croc brain is your fight-or flight-mechanism.

This early warning system still functions today by filtering every single piece of information you get, every situation you face, and every message you receive.

The croc brain's primary function is to keep you safe. It knows you will feel safer in a group situation with people who share similar values and beliefs to yourself. This stems from the survival of the fittest, when living in groups for protection was essential. It aims is to keep you safe within your comfort zone.

The croc brain is also lazy. It lives by three simple rules: If there is not an immediate threat, ignore it. If it's not new, unique, exciting, or alarming, ignore it. If it IS new, unique, exciting or alarming, summarise and deal with the information as quickly as possible. If this can't be done – ignore and dispose of it.

This means that up to 90 percent of information is quickly discarded and forgotten before it has had the opportunity to reach your brain's higher level of consciousness.

Therefore, for your communication to filter through the croc brain, it must be new, unique, exciting, or alarming. And it must be easily summarised, so the croc brain can pass it over with the least amount of effort.

The palemammalian brain is the limbic system, which developed after the croc brain. It is the part of your brain dealing with emotions. It determines the meaning of things. It understands social situations and how people relate to you in your life. It understands status. Its role is to keep you functioning in society. It governs the kind of people who are attracted to you and vice versa.

Your belief systems are stored in the very deep limbic part of the brain. Your belief system also has a filtering system. For instance, if you believe making money in a recession is difficult, you won't see the opportunity to make money because you believe you can't make money during a recession. If you changed your belief system to that of believing you can make money during a recession, things would change. You would start to see the opportunities to make money and have the courage to take action on these.

What is important to understand about the limbic system is that it does not have language. You can't change limiting beliefs using language because the information is not stored as words. It is stored as emotions.

To change limiting beliefs, you have to start working on the emotional part of the brain through feelings. For some people this can be a painful process and hurt deeply, causing people to back away and not want to go there. But it is necessary to do the work on your belief system if it is to become supportive of the success you want.

When emotions rise, your brain will deliberately work to suppress these feelings. It will begin to use aversion tactics, sabotaging your potential success. Remember: your brain wants to keep you safe. It will do this subconsciously. For instance, if you dread giving a presentation to a large group, your brain's fight and flight mechanism will respond by giving you symptoms of anxiety, such as shaking, or feeling faint. These are natural feelings, but by nature you will want to run away. By bringing these feelings into consciousness, you are in a position to explore where the feelings are manifesting from and be able to deal with them.

The third and largest part of your brain is the neomammalian, or neocortex; size wise, it makes up approximately five-sixths of your entire brain.

This part of the brain is where language, speech, writing, and logical thinking take place. You plan your future and solve problems using this part of your brain. It is incredibly intelligent, but completely emotionless. It does not care about social situations. It is not good at managing survival.

The rules of the neocortex are: if it's confusing, it doesn't want to deal with it. If it's not visual, it doesn't want to engage with it. If it's abstract and not concrete, then the croc brain has to deal with it. The neocortex does not want to receive old problems. The croc brain is your gatekeeper.

For your communication to reach the neocortex, it has to be done in a certain way. The information needs to be fast, visual, concrete, novel, and high contrast.

Does it matter which part of your brain is used in decision-making?

In his book The Naked Brain, Richard Restak explains that when people are forced to make a decision using the neocortex, they take longer and tend to over-think the decision. And when they do, the decision is often of a lower quality.

When people dither about whether or not to buy your products and services, using excuses such as needing to check with their partner, not being sure and having to think about it, or saying they will get back to you, the decision making is often taking place in the neocortex.

In contrast, when a decision is made by the croc and the limbic brain it is more likely to be an instant decision, a gut reaction with an emotional connection. Your prospect knows it feels right. The excuses of not wanting to buy disappear. This is often a higher quality decision.

When sourcing your business angels, the connection happens in the croc and limbic part of the brain. It is an emotional and intuitive connection. It instantly feels right.

I'm sure you'll agree that the amazing way your brain is wired, how it interprets and processes information, its circuitry evolving at an ever-increasing speed in our digital communications age, is truly magical.

> # The brain is a wonderful organ; it starts working the moment you get up in the morning and does not stop until you get into the office.
>
> ## Robert Frost

Keys to Powering Up Your Communication

- Your amazing brain receives a minimum of two million pieces of information per second.
- Ninety percent of all information received is immediately discarded.
- The reptilian or 'croc' brain filters all information. It is your brain's gatekeeper. It is your fight-or-flight mechanism.
- The function of the reptilian 'croc' brain is to keep you safe. It will seek out people, groups, or situations with similar values and beliefs to you.
- The palemammalian 'limbic' brain storing your belief systems does not have language. It has emotion. Beliefs can not be changed using words.
- Decisions made by the reptilian and palemammalian 'limbic' brain tend to be far superior and instant in comparison to those made by the neocortex.
- Your brain is set to keep you in your comfort zone, for safety, rather than to make you successful.
- Business angels connect on an emotional, intuitive level, an energy frequency via feelings and intuition. In other words, when the student is ready, the teacher will appear.

Note: A very special thank you to Dorina Lanza for your help, assistance and personal contribution to my gaining this information.

Wendy Howard

You build on failure.
You use it as a stepping stone.
Close the door on the past.
You don't try to
forget the mistakes,
but you don't dwell on it.
You don't let it have
any of your energy,
or any of your time,
or any of your space.

Johnny Cash

Chapter Eleven

Lighting Up Your Amazing Soul Path
Freedom from the Veil of Illusion

Are you now beginning to understand how and why there is often a big disconnect between your current path and that of your natural, intended soul path?

And why, no matter how hard you work, unless you re-learn new ways of doing things and reset your brain, you will always return back to where you started, facing the same old problems and similar situations?

It's like having a rewind-repeat button in your life, but you don't realise you're trapped in the scenario. It's similar to the story in the romantic comedy Groundhog Day, where a wacky weatherman is forced to relive one strange day over and over again until he gets it right.

In life, you live in a similar way, subconsciously repeating the behaviours you're programmed with, until finally, you discover there is another way. You align with your soul path. The world becomes a brighter, more meaningful place. You finally get it right.

One of the twentieth century's most influential spiritual teachers, George Gurdijeff, explains it like this: "You are in prison. If you wish to get out of prison, the first thing you must do is realise that you are in prison. If you think you are free, then you can't escape."

George believed most humans live their lives in a state of hypnotic 'waking sleep', repeating the same patterns over and over.

But, he believed it is still possible to transcend to a higher consciousness to achieve our full human potential.

Today's intense magnetic pull of the new feminine economy powerfully draws us towards transcending to a higher consciousness, to achieving our fullest potential, while giving something meaningful back. It's an evolutionary change and you must look out for the subtle signs of where to go, and who to connect with.

In life it's as if when you go about finding your path to success, you're actually oblivious to being in an trancelike, hypnotic, waking, sleep and unaware that in reality, you're slowly being sucked towards yet another prison door.

When you're in that disconnected place, it's as if an invisible veil is clouding your judgement. You feel as though there is something wonderful on the other side while you remain detached in a labyrinth of illusion and confusion.

Disconnected, disillusioned, resentful; it's the illusion created by your ego.

The Hindu-Buddhist concept Maya explains this to some extent. Maya relates to the constant movement of the universe, powerfully masking the phenomenal world of reality, which can only be perceived behind a 'veil of illusion'.

In Sanskrit, the word Maya derives from the idea that the mundane physical and mental reality of everyday consciousness has clouded our perception of being part of a bigger whole. We choose to attach ourselves to our injuries, our stories, and our emotions. We are in fact removed from our natural greatness.

In Kabbalah, the Tree Of Life is a diagram representing both the process by which the universe came into being and the path to higher power. The Veil of Paroketh lies between the upper realms and the lower realms as a symbolic portal through which consciousness must traverse when travelling upward towards the Tree Of Life, to reach a conscious union with your soul.

The Veil of Paroketh is the barrier between your ego and your soul. Below the veil, the ego believes it is your soul's identity. Paroketh is called the veil of illusion because everything that lies below the veil is an illusion.

Your soul resides on the other side, which is true reality. When taking steps to passing through the veil, gaining your connection of wholeness and love of your own soul, the ego will reflect back any unresolved fears and desires. These will be projected into forms that seem real to you.

What actually happens is when you feel sure you're on the right path and feel as though you are under no illusion as to the right direction for you, infact, you may still be lost in an illusion that is made up of your own preconceptions. So you may be out of touch with reality of your true situation.

Raising the veil of illusion and reconnecting with reality.

To raise the veil of illusion and reconnect with reality there is a need to experience a state of liberation by letting go and believing in oneself, while gaining freedom from the confines of limiting beliefs by making the connection to your soul source. This is all part of the heart-centred entrepreneur's journey. Initially, not everyone is clear on what their soul source is, or what their direction should be, or what they should be doing in business to give them the fulfillment they're searching for.

Initially, take time out to mull over your ideas. Explore what you were good at as a child. What brought you happiness then? If you were starting your life over again, what would you love to do? What would you include in your life? What would you leave out? These are some of the initial areas to explore.

Secondly, give it time to nurture your ideas. There is so much expectation to be fabulously famous and make a big six or seven figure income virtually overnight. That again is just an illusion. It's not impossible, but the reality is that for the majority of entrepreneurs it takes time, energy, and business knowledge to do that. In the first instance, I'd always recommend looking at how you might start to bring your ideas to life while still doing your day job. Only give that up when your business can sufficiently support you to do that.

Doing things this way, it will enable you to build up your self-belief that you can do what you've chosen to do and earn income from it. Subconsciously, you will learn to think, act, feel, and communicate on a completely different level. You will be enthusiastic in your work and this will be expressed energetically and charismatically when you meet people.

Everything will start to change. What seemed impossible becomes possible. Clients will be attracted to you and willing to pay higher prices than your competition. They will stay loyal and remain devout followers. Your personal and business chakras will be strong. You will attract your business angels at exactly the right time you need them. Step through the veil of illusion and get ready to rock your world!

> Change will not come if we wait for some other person or some other time.
> We are the ones we've been waiting for.
> We are the change that we seek.
>
> Barack Obama

Wendy Howard

Success does not consist in never making mistakes but in never making the same one a second time.

George Bernard Shaw

Chapter Twelve

Your Cells Have Memories Too

David's Story

I've known David since our school days; although he was in a different class and a year above me, we connected (that energy thing again).

At school, David had difficulty with reading and writing. Leaving school at the first opportunity - at age 15 - he could barely read or write. He believed his parents when they said, "You're stupid; school is a waste of time for the likes of you, so go and get a job."

David did get a job. He went into civil engineering, excelling in driving large JCB machinery, excavating, building, and land drainage. Within five years, he'd put a deposit down on his first JCB, realising he could make more money working for himself than for someone else.

Within ten years, David had established a thriving business with a turnover of over £2.6 million a year. He now employed his father and two brothers in the business.

If a friend fell on hard times, David helped them out by giving them a monetary handout, or by offering them a job, even if he had to source more work to be able to employ them. A second home with a swimming pool in beautiful Spain and a top of the range Mercedes in the drive were the rewards of his success.

Forty-three years after leaving school, David called me from a hospital bed following a heart attack. Thankfully, he'd managed to call for help after feeling ill with excruciating chest pain as he was coming out of the shower. Fifteen more minutes without help, and he would have died.

David's ill health, brought on by stress, stemmed from a number of serious business mistakes he'd made in recent years. His business was on the brink of insolvency. A large divorce settlement demanded by his second wife lost him the home in Spain and the majority of their savings in their joint bank account. To raise capital, David remortgaged his original home and began to sell off large assets of the company as the recession brought a slump in business. When he became unable to continue to employ his brothers and father in the business, it caused a family rift.

David was now angry and bitter, complaining that no one was prepared to help him, although they'd been quite happy to take everything he'd offered them during the profitable years.

As I listened, David related his story of having missed his children growing up because of the long hours he'd spent at work. He'd not had the exotic holidays or taken long breaks from the business like his brothers, because he was the responsible one who could not take time off. David's brothers had solid relationships and nice homes, which were all paid for, whereas David's home was at risk due to his remortgaging to keep the company solvent. Personal relationships did not last, no matter how generous he was with his money, because he always had to work, taking full responsibility for everyone.

As his anger diminished, David acknowledged he'd made mistakes that had cost him and his business dearly.

His now elderly father and brothers had made their feelings very clear: he'd been foolish with money, making stupid and unnecessary mistakes. He'd lost them their jobs and future security.

Then we got to the crux of it. "Nobody knows what it feels like to be told by your father at nine years old that you're stupid because you're incapable of reading and writing a simple sentence. Work harder; you're just being lazy. You are the stupidest boy I've ever known."

Dyslexia wasn't recognised forty years ago. Bright kids were often labelled stupid, not receiving the help they needed. David had spent a lifetime working hard to prove he wasn't stupid and to show his family that he could be someone.

But David hadn't dealt with the underlying issues or the accompanying emotional trauma embedded into his cells - until now, when forced to do so.

What is cell memory?

Cell memory is a term given to pain, inflammation, or a medical condition that can be identified from a particular period in a person's life. In David's case, the cell memory stemmed from when he was aged nine.

Labels such as 'mind', 'body', and 'spirit' make it easier to understand your multi-dimensional existence on earth. Imagine if you could magnify your cells enough to see the atoms underlying them, and you will see that you are made up of subtle bundles of 'info-energy.' This info-energy comprises physical, mental, and emotional data, which comes from all of your life experiences, genetic heritage, and past generations. Nothing escapes this data capture. It is your unique blueprint of who you are.

Your cellular memory is the collective energy field generated by individual cell memories. It operates behind the scenes of your subconscious mind.

How does cellular memory work?

Your cellular memory predisposes or programmes you to perceive and behave a certain way as thoughts and feelings manifest within your consciousness.

Using the analogy of a computer, the cellular memory is your database. The files within your database are the cell memories. Everything that has ever happened to you is recorded in the cells of your body in a similar way to files being stored on a computer.

In this way, it influences your relationship to everything and anything that is happening. It affects the way you perform a task, how you react to stress and handle emotional challenges in your present circumstances.

Your conscious and unconscious patterns of behaviour are all stored here. Any unproductive patterns impair your ability to feel well, happy, and healthy, or to achieve goals and fulfill your destiny.

What happens when memories are suppressed?

Dr. Candace Pert, PhD in pharmacology and author of Molecules of Emotion, says, "Repressing emotions can only be causative of disease. Failure to find effective ways to express negative emotions causes you to stew in your own juices."

According to Pert, the key is found in the complex molecules called neuropeptides, including endorphins.

These are the means for cell communications, including brain-to-brain messages, body-to-body messages, and body-to-brain messages.

Variations and changes occur, reflecting variations in your emotions throughout the day. The kind and number of emotion-linked neuropeptides available at receptor sites of cells influences your probability of staying well or getting sick.

It has long been recognised that there is a link between repressed emotions and the location in the body the imbalance or disease begins to manifest.

In Oriental medicine, each organ or gland has one or more emotions that influence it. The emotional trauma will most likely begin to manifest the imbalance in a corresponding organ or gland. Emotional toxicity plays an equal and perhaps a more dominant role in achieving optimum health.

Health issues include anxiety, fear, sleeplessness, fear of success or failure, and any kind of negative repeating patterns. The cause can be inherited ancestral issues or many other energetic causes.

Ancestral issues may arise from many generations past.

Even though your family may have been healthy, wealthy, and wise, it is possible for a strong negative influence from many generations back to impact a member of the present generation, leading to depression, lack of motivation, failure, or choosing an apparently illogical career or activity.

Financial issues and limiting beliefs are frequently ancestral in nature from many generations past.

Past energies of slavery, oppression, poverty, famines, domination, shame, and guilt can reappear in later generations and at a minimum can cause conflict with your goals and desires, leading to depression, dramatic changes, and more. All these possibilities can normally be identified and rectified with energy healing.

David's case is particularly interesting, albeit sad because in many ways, he is still that nine-year-old kid, facing shame for not being able to read or write, spending a lifetime feeling stupid, still seeking his father's approval by working hard. In business David proved he could achieve more success than most people will ever achieve. But his damaged cell blueprint would always rise up at some point to jeopardise his success because he had not dealt with the underlying issues.

David's story highlights the importance of incorporating energy healing while building your business chakras.

Inheriting cell memories from previous generations.

There is more to David's story, which raises deeper issues. David's mother arrived in the United Kingdom in 1962 escaping the military coup in Burma. At this time, the United Nations and several organisations reported consistent systematic human rights violations in that country. These included genocide, the use of child soldiers, systematic rape, child labour, slavery, human trafficking and a lack of freedom of speech.

Can you imagine for a few moments how terrifying it must have been for David's mother in oppressive Burma during that time, and the communication difficulties she faced arriving in the United Kingdom with little ability to read or write the English language.

Does this not raise the question as to the probability of David inheriting memory cells from a previous generation, namely his mother's? Coupled with the expectation of the oldest child being the breadwinner, as is the culture in Burma, and the need to work hard to please his father, the pressure on David was immense.

The truth is, it was always written in David's blueprint that unless he dealt with the deeper issues they would always come through and manifest as problems at some point in his life. And sadly, they did.

> Do not dwell in the past,
> do not dream of the future,
> concentrate the mind
> on the present moment.
>
> Buddha

The gift of fantasy
has meant more to me
than my talent for absorbing
positive knowledge.

Albert Einstein

Chapter Thirteen

You ARE The Hero In Your Story
Awaken Your Hungry Soul

What games did you play as a child? Can you remember? Were you Batman or Robin, one of the caped crusaders? Wonder Woman, or the Six Million Dollar Man? Perhaps you scaled the garden walls as Spider Man, or practiced the art of sophistication as James Bond with an imaginary Martini, shaken, not stirred?

As a child I'm sure you recall escaping into a wonderful fantasy world where you became the hero or heroine in your story. As children, we do this naturally. We play games. We stand confident, centre stage. We naturally become greater, stronger, more dynamic.

As a child, releasing your inner hero, entering a magical fantasy world is natural. Who doesn't want to be Tom Cruise in Top Gun? Or Keira Knightley in Pirates of the Caribbean? Who says you can't be that person and do what they do? As a child, the question never comes up.

You get into the game as your imaginary story plays out; you belong and you're part of it. You feel energised, alive, at one with the world; your inner hero always wins the day.

As a sleepy, fulfilled child, you headed home at sunset for tea with a burning inner glow. You sleep well at night, rising refreshed to embrace yet another heroic play-filled day. Hearts filled with the joys of summertime.

Then, as your early play days moved into adoration for teenage idols, who did you worship then?

It was the gentle melody of dreamy doe-eyed Donny Osmond's Puppy Love pulling at my younger sister's heartstrings. I was more the rock chick, bopping along to Tina Turner's Nut Bush City Limits.

Isn't it amazing how a song or a piece of music immediately takes you back to those happy, carefree times as if it were yesterday?

Moving on to college, university, or into your first job, who or what inspired you then? Was it a rock star, a sports person, or an academic? Who was your first love? What was it like to feel that way?

Oh the bliss of those memories. For me, with more than a hint of melancholy, I recall my last summer of teenage freedom. I spent it cruising in a borrowed old black Mini, racing along the sea front of golden sands in beautiful Torquay, lined with palm trees, singing along to the song Hi Ho Silver Lining.

Not a care in the world. No money in the bank. No responsibilities. Just a beautiful, enjoyable, sunny, happy time, before life took over.

But what happened to that creative, confident young spirit? What inspired you back then?

Leaders inspire us, even in movies. They give us a sense of purpose and belonging. You do not need to be bribed or convinced to follow a great leader. You just do it. But what is it that entices you to follow?
Why do you want to belong? Is it to support the leader?
No, it's not that at all.

The reason you want to follow a great leader is because something has stirred inside of you connecting and awakening your hungry soul, which has been starved of soul-nourishment since life got in the way.

As a child you played out the hero. But as you grew, you became detached from who you were meant to be. Life took over, and those blissful heroic days became a distant childhood memory.

But somewhere deep inside, your soul remembers how it felt to be hero for a day. Your soul still longs to feel that way again. In doing so, you will do anything to follow the leader who touches and awakens your soul.

It brings you back to life.

Hero worship, gurus, and being aware of the vulnerable soul.

This is why we have guru worship. Your hungry soul will pay premium prices to follow the leader who instills a deep sense of belonging.

Gurus, charismatic leaders know clients stay loyal when the hungry soul is nurtured. By sharing their expertise, lighting your dark path, it feels like you are coming home to a warm, soothing bath.

You will fight for limited places and exclusive deals because your primitive tribal instinct is urging you towards a safe and reassuring place where you no longer have to survive on your own.

But at this time, you must take care. Your soul is vulnerable and hasn't played the hero for some time, possibly since childhood.

When it is awakened, it wants to live and to feel that extraordinarily powerful way it did when you were an innocent child hero.

In earnest, your hungry soul naturally reaches out to the nearest flame of desire. So begins the hero worship trap. Searching for the get-rich-quick, the faster or easier solution, or the quick fix to your business or life problems.

Attending talks and seminars is essential to lifelong learning. After all, it is a primitive drive to do so. Many leaders are hard working individuals and offer incredible value to help you grow and overcome barriers.

It only becomes a problem when you spend your life and hard-earned cash chasing dreams, worshipping gurus, longing for your big break, but never quite making it yourself.

There comes a time when you must step out of the hero worship glow, release your leader within and do it for yourself. You must find the courage while denying the voice of your inner critic. It's your time to step up, step out, and finally get noticed.

So who should you choose to work with? Who can you trust to be your guide? When do you know you've found the right mentor? How do you attract your business angels when you need them?

The heart, not the head, must be the guide.
Arthur Erickson

Following Footsteps in the Snow

I'll share with you a story that will resonate with your ability to making the right choice in seeking a mentor. It's called Footsteps in the Snow.

It goes like this:

Imagine you have a journey to make. This journey will take you on a mountain path, covered by very deep, powdery snow, glistening in the sunlight. Your breath freezes in midair as you strap on your ski shoes, intending to make the trek across the mountain to the yet unknown place waiting for you on the other side.

You know if you go on this journey alone, you will be the first person to walk this path after a heavy snowfall. New snow is very difficult to walk through. You have no map. You do not know the path. There are no footsteps to follow. You could get stuck in unfamiliar territory. In this terrain, you are at risk of getting lost. You could even die.

This is the path of the lone entrepreneur, the people trying to work it out for themselves without seeking the help they need. It is the hardest route. It has the highest risk. There is no map or guarantee you will ever get to your destination. Very few ever succeed on this path.

If, on the other hand, you take a few moments observing the landscape, you may look closely and discover some tracks. You can see they are very old tracks, not very clear - at times, fading out altogether.

Fresh snow drifting on the winds is obscuring the path in places. Poor weather dims your view ahead, so you don't see the person who's made these tracks. Or if you do, they are so far ahead they won't notice you are there. They won't look back or come get you if you falter along the path.

Taking this path, it will be difficult for you to make progress. You are at risk of losing sight of the path altogether. The person who has gone before you is too far ahead to be of any real comfort or guidance to you. This is the guru worship route. This is a hard route to follow. Failure is high, and few make it to the other side.

So you decide to weigh up your options. While you're deciding what to do, someone comes along, virtually beside you, very confident in their approach as they take off across the snowy terrain. They are smiling. They know the route well and they know where the guru ahead is likely to be heading. They turn around, giving you a friendly wave, beckoning you to follow them. They wait for you to catch up.

When you do, you find the tracks made in the fresh snow are easy to follow. You simply place one foot in front of the other; stepping into the imprints made by the person ahead is easy. Should you slip or fall, they are close enough to turn back, helping you get back on your feet again. If you go off track, they will stop and holler at you: 'Danger ahead', getting you back on the right path.

This is the easiest route. This is the person you should follow, who's just a short way ahead of you, but not so far ahead that you can't see where the route is. Following in their track is easy. They know the way. Importantly, they are not so far ahead that you will be left behind. They still empathise with what it feels like to be where you are right now. They know the way you must go. This is the person you should choose to work with.

By following the right people, being in the right place and at the right time, step by step you will soon find yourself bathing in the limelight. In turn, your fans will want to follow in your footsteps.

Think for a few moments how great that will make you feel.

> Outstanding leaders
> go out of their way to
> boost the self-esteem
> of their people.
> If people believe
> in themselves, it's amazing
> what they can accomplish.
>
> Sam Walton

Let no man
in the world
live in delusion.
Without a Guru
none can cross over
to the other shore.

Guru Nanak

Chapter Fourteen

When Harry Meets Sally
Motivational Secrets in Guru Land

Let's explore guru land a little bit more, shall we? It's such an interesting place to be.

Have you ever wondered what motivates people to leap from their seats in a seminar, send them rushing to the back of the room to grab one of those elite (but always very limited) places on an often overpriced ticket?

I'm sure if you've been an entrepreneur for a while, then you've witnessed this happening in guru land. It's that Harry Meets Sally moment when you've just got to have what she's having. The carefully crafted educational session, slowly seducing you into that moment when the big value boot sale offer takes place. And wham. You're hooked in before it's gone.

Credit card in hand, you're on your feet racing with the crowd to grab one of the last remaining available places to work with the guru who's woken your inner hero.

How do they do it?

Why are you motivated to respond?

Here's the secret. It's partly explained by looking at the four instinctive motivational drives, which are rooted in your brain's survival instincts.

1. The Motivational Drive to Acquire

At the most primitive level, you are motivated to acquire the basics of food and shelter, keeping you alive. Back in cave land, you killed an animal one day, ate some of it, and learned how to dry the rest out, saving it for a time when food would be scarce.

We still use these skills today, although they're somewhat more sophisticated, with our large supermarkets and home fridges and freezers. The reality is, if a crisis comes up, you'd still store your basics to ensure you'd stay alive. It works in the same way as people who've invested in survival shelters storing basic needs in times of war, or by having a basement especially converted and equipped to ensure their survival should there be a holocaust. It is your primitive 'croc' survival brain at work again.

At this basic level, you also possess a 'positional' drive. This is where you buy things of status to show the world who and what you are. This might be the designer handbag or clothing you wear, the car you drive or the house you purchase in a select part of the country. It has a certain basic importance at a primitive level.

2. The Motivational Drive to Bond

When your ancestors lived in caves, it was essential to be part of a tribe for protection and survival. Your motivational drive to bond and belong to a community derives from that time. It didn't die just because you've moved on from cave times.

The tribal bond instinct leads you to join groups, to be where the action is. This is why you want to be in the company of like-minded people: because it makes you feel safe. This is why mastermind and networking groups are successful. If a group resonates with your problem and already has like-minded people as members, it is likely you will want to join.

3. The Motivational Drive to Learn

At cave level, the more you learned then the more survival knowledge and skills you gained made it more likely you were to stay alive. There was a need to be consistent, to maintain order and predictability.

Without a strong drive to learn, you would be vulnerable and unlikely to survive for long. In cave days, it really was a case of survival of the fittest. You either learned to survive or you died.

You still have an active primal survival instinct urging you to maintain lifelong learning.

4. The Drive to Defend

You also have a natural drive to defend when feeling threatened. For instance, you will naturally want to defend your home if you come face to face with an intruder. You will stand up for your family and friends if you feel they're getting a raw deal or being bullied. You will fiercely stand by your beliefs and get into a heated argument if it's something you feel strongly about.

How many times have you listened to a debate or watched Question Time on TV and observed the opposing sides, both vehemently defending their point of view on a sensitive subject? The drive to defend is strong.

You too will defend your ideas and your way of thinking. It's part of your innate survival instinct. Gurus and slick marketers know this, but there's more.

While the four motivational drives explain why we are driven to acquire, bond, learn and defend, studies in social intelligence and social biology have identified:

i. We will chase what moves away from us.

If you see something slipping away, when time is running out and you've got to make a decision or miss out, then you are much more likely to want it.

Again, it's a primal instinct very much like when my dog Shadow sees a cat. He's got to chase it the moment it starts to move away. If the cat sat still and didn't move but was in the same place every day he'd ignore it.

ii. We want what it appears we cannot have.

You will yearn for the Bahamian beach lifestyle, the exclusive hotel, the first class business seat, the millionaire lifestyle, the adoration of the crowd, or an opportunity to bathe in the limelight.

This is the same reason we have a saying that the grass is always greener. It is natural to want what we do not have, when it is appealingly presented to us.

iii. We will place value on things that are difficult to obtain.

If an offer states that you have to go through a selection process before being accepted then this adds value. You are more likely to be motivated into taking action because you are presented with something difficult to obtain. This is the reason why many offers are set up asking you to qualify before being accepted onto a course, or to be given one of a limited number of seats available.

Now do you see how a carefully crafted offer triggers your motivational drives? By further sprinkling in the traits identified by social intelligence and social biology, you often can't resist buying from the guru with the right motivational cocktail for you to buy from them. It works!

Gurus all had to start from a place not dissimilar to you or I. Often it's not that they have a greater product or service than you or I; it has far more to do with the ability to market their products and services well by triggering those motivational buttons to get you to buy.

I'm sure you'll agree guru land is an interesting, exciting, and an educational place to be. Watch, listen, and learn.

> You are never too old
> to set another goal or
> to dream a new dream.
>
> C. S. Lewis

Wendy Howard

Take the first step in faith.
You don't have to
see the whole staircase,
just take the first step.

Martin Luther King, Jr.

Chapter Fifteen

Your Magical Destiny Path
One Step for Mankind

How did Neil Armstrong feel during the first moon-landing mission I wonder? Did he ever doubt himself or those behind the expedition? Did he ever feel afraid he'd not return to see his loved ones ever again?

I'm sure on his historic journey "taking one giant leap for mankind," Neil faced many emotions, perhaps at times almost paralysing ones. But his successful mission secured his place in history while adding to the great universal knowledge database.

Only three percent right, 97 percent wrong, and you will still arrive at your destination.

I'm sure much of Neil's confidence and reassurance on achieving success on the Apollo mission lay in his carefully calculated margin of error. This meant that Neil was only ever three percent of the time on target and 97 percent of the time off course, and he was still able to reach his destination and land on the moon. Neil Armstrong was very much a trail-blazer to the many space missions taking place since that time.

Similarly, today's entrepreneurs are very much trail-blazers. There is no map in the age of technology and new feminine business economy. We're going to places we haven't been before or could even imagine in the past. We can only rely on a carefully calculated margin of error based on prior achievements, creativity, and intuition.

By seeking out help from the great masters, the business angels who've gone before and carved a path, you will be able to share their knowledge and experience to calculate your own business margin of error in our technologically driven age. Then all you have to do is keep your destination as a vision, and let your magical destiny path unfold before you.

Ignore your doubt demons, dispel your fears, and slay your inner dragons along the way. When you let go of doubts, fears, and negative thinking, you nurture the leader within and you become who you were meant to be before life's junk got in your way.

Keep your focus on your destination, let go of negativity and be assured that your margin of error will keep you within safe boundaries and on course. Believe in yourself as you already have the answers inside of you.

The Inside-Out approach

Positioning your business from the soul is the inside-out approach rather than the outside-in approach. Everything you and your team do or say, your products, services, marketing, culture, how you look and present yourself and your business, must be consistent, congruent, and authentic. When you have total belief in what you are selling, you will feel passionate. Your belief will be powerful and your energy magnetic.

Ben & Jerry's famous ice cream is an amazing inside-out success story. Let's take a look at the inside-out approach in practice.

Ben & Jerry's Recipe for Success
Key Ingredient One:

A great core story. Ben and Jerry are lifetime friends sharing a very special bond: they both hated running at school, but loved food. Ben failed to keep a job, and Jerry failed to get into medical school. With just $5, together they did a correspondence course in ice cream making. They opened their first shop in a dilapidated gas station in downtown Burlington, Vermont.

Their popular ice cream concoctions, loved by their local community, developed because Ben had no sense of taste. He relied on what he described as 'mouth feel', leading to chunky chocolate and fruit and nuts becoming their signature products.

At the start they were not good at business. It folded after two months. They hung a sign outside of the building saying, "We're closed to figure out whether we're making any money." They discovered they were not.

But they had gained a lot of valuable knowledge from their experience and instead they began wholesaling pints of ice cream out of Ben's VW camper van. The rest is history.

Key Ingredient Two: Communicating 'soul to soul'.

'At Ben and Jerry's we're all about making the best possible ice cream in the nicest possible way'.

The business is founded on and dedicated to a sustainable corporate concept of linked prosperity in their three-part social, product, and economic mission statement.

In addition, underlying their mission is the determination to seek new and creative ways of addressing all three parts, while holding a deep respect for the communities of which they are a part.

Key Ingredient Three:

Attracting a tribal following. Ben & Jerry's actively invite you to apply online to become part of their growing community success story with regular competitions, giving something back—helping local communities leap out from the very canvas of their business.

Success elements

- A willingness to learn by viewing mistakes as opportunities for positive change.
- Overcoming obstacles, by starting with just US $5.
- Not giving up when it wasn't working. Instead, stopping, and reviewing their business model.
- Retaining the sense of fun they had as kids. Their branding emits an essence of fun and creativity with childish font, bright colours, pictures, and online games.
- Strong values, ethical leadership, and community create a sense of belonging to something far greater. Tom & Jerry's has soul!

Take inspiration from Ben & Jerry's success story to find your magical destiny path:

What is your core story? Write this out.

What lies at the heart of your business? Get clear on this.

Is your business aligned with your soul? Honestly?

Do you communicate your message from the soul?

If not, how can you do this?

Is your soul energy blazing a trail to attract your tribe?

If not, how can you light the trail?

Miracles
happen everyday,
change your
perception of
what a miracle is
and you'll see them
all around you.

Jon Bon Jovi

Chapter Sixteen

Embracing Evolutionary Change
A Database in the Corridors of Time

At times, does it seem as if you are still that tiny particle of sand on the beach of the great universal vortex, waiting to be transformed? You know in your heart you have a part to play, a contribution to give. But as soon as you build your sandcastle on the beach, life's vast ocean sweeps in and washes your dreams and aspirations away.

I'll let you in on a secret. There is a space in life's ocean where miracles really do happen. In this space, there is a place waiting for your valuable contribution. The universe has a greater importance: the bigger picture perspective.

In the turbulence of our crazy weather, natural disasters, and life's personal up and downs, we question, we reason, we want to comprehend. Why is this happening now?

What we often don't acknowledge is that in our digital communications age, we're building on centuries of previous knowledge that has led us to be where we are today.

Think of this knowledge like a computer database. As each century passes, knowledge from that century is being added to this database. This way, we're continually growing and expanding.

This huge universal database stores centuries of great vats of universal knowledge and energies, which are known as vortexes.

Using the analogy of corridors of time for this huge storage of knowledge, which is passed down through the centuries, imagine each time-based corridor as having an energy source travelling throughout the universes, holding knowledge within the many vortexes in space.

Every cycle the universal creation passes through leaves an imprint of evolution within the membranes of the corridors of time.

Within this knowledge base lies the contribution of every great master who has gone before. All knowledge contributions are stored, along with the imprints of creation, in the various stages of evolution.

This is the database of everything from the beginning of the big bang, the present and the future, everything and nothing. It's a pure energy force flowing throughout the creation of space and time. It is the blueprint of creation.

We can think of this pure energy as a universal light source of consciousness. Within this light consciousness, all knowledge is born; all knowledge of past events is stored and can be recalled within its evolutionary cycle.

Every great master who has ever lived has left his or her contribution as an imprint. These cycles of consciousness store the evolutionary records of everyone and everything. You, too, will leave an imprint. Your contribution matters greatly. Never doubt that.

Knowledge contributions from the great masters accumulate to our greater knowing and belonging. Everyone from the great Greek philosopher Aristotle, born in Stagira in 384 BC, with his contributions to physics, poetry, zoology, logic, rhetoric, politics, government, ethics, and biology; to Sir Issac Newton, the physicist, mathematician, astronomer, alchemist, and natural philosopher. His contribution to the development of science is a special one. He is best known for the development of universal gravitation and the three laws of motion.

Albert Einstein, one of the most notable physicists of all time, was identified as having a learning disability in childhood. He could not talk until he was three years old or read a book until the age of eight. Yet he became the Nobel Prize winner for his contribution to physics. Einstein's theory of relativity is considered to be a revolutionary development in the world of physics.

Stephen Hawking is considered the greatest scientist of the twentieth century - after Einstein. His Big Bang theory and Black Hole theory have attracted the attention of the world. Even his failing body and paralysis did not prevent him from his research and writing his book, A Brief History of Time.

Likewise, we all have a contribution to make to this growing body of energy and knowledge. This is your time to add to the collective universal powers of thought. Your valuable contribution as a heart-centred entrepreneur has never been more important than it is today. Indeed, it is your duty to use the power of communication available to everyone to contribute wholly.

If you do not
change direction,
you may end up
where you are heading.

Lao Tzu

Chapter Seventeen

Can You Feel It?
Shift of Universal Consciousness

Change is upon us. People are daily becoming more aware as evidenced by the many uprising events taking place in our world. For instance, the recent events in Egypt and Ukraine where people have banded together in protest of what they believe to be better ways. This is all to do with a global shift in consciousness towards oneness. People are no longer wanting to be dictated to but rather to be open and able to question and trust in their inner guidance.

In a way, the universal consciousness being emitted is similar to the energies creating the spectacular performance of the northern lights. I observed this amazing phenomenon throughout my time living in Norway and during my travels through the very mystical Iceland. To witness and soak in the sheer magnificence of this natural phenomenon, one gets a sense of belonging, a reconnection with the energies of life.

On a far greater scale than the northern lights, the universal consciousness, being emitted as a continuous shift of energy, fluctuates within its own vibration, bringing changes throughout space and time. On earth we observe these changes as natural phenomena taking place.

Changes occur within a cyclic pattern, a formation of universal energy structure, which many people cannot physically observe, although they feel it when a disturbance is created.

When certain cycles change within the energy transformation of universal creation, then the corridors of time are opened. It is through universal consciousness when a major cycle is ready to transform itself into a new cycle.

We are currently witnessing such an evolutionary disturbance during our lifetime. We're being drawn towards universal transformational and evolutionary change and it happening right now.

Many are highly sensitive to this current energy flow and disturbance. This is why many people are searching for something more meaningful in their lives right now, while others, in denial, may remain trapped in a materialistic but painfully disconnected physical world.

Whilst embracing the beginning of this new cycle, there has been much speculation and misinterpretation of the Mayan calendar, which skeptics attempted to interpret as the end of the world. Actually it meant something else.

The Mayans had a very complex calendar that included planetary observations, which are not part of our calendar. The cycle of the Mayan calendar takes 2,012 years to complete. Our calendar cycle takes just one year. But what both calendars have in common is that on the last day of the current calendar, it begins a new cycle.

So on 22 December 2012, the Mayans did not predict the end of the world. Their calendar is continuous and starts a new cycle, which will last another 2,012 years. We are at the start of this new time period cycle.

New energy formations and a shift in consciousness occur as the corridors of time open. This new cycle transmits new energy formations, creating a new cycle of universal consciousness, which can affect all aspects of nature. With it comes a shift in consciousness and new evolutionary change.

The more people who become aware of this consciousness and its various energy patterns, the more stable the earth will become in alignment with that of the higher consciousness of this universal source.

When this energy is activated, the energy formation is projected onto the planet. In turn, new geography patterns form; shifts of ley lines and meridians begin to occur, affecting nature. This explains somewhat why our weather is erratic, earthquakes and tsunamis are more frequent, and world events are chaotic and unpredictable.

The concept of ley lines as cosmic forces of energy penetrating and leaving the earth vertically at nodes, or power centres originating outside of the earth was first discovered by Alfred Watkins. Watkins also drew on earlier ideas about alignments, in particular the work of English astronomer Norman Lockyer, who argues that ancient alignments might be oriented sunrise to sunset as solstices. Ley lines along with water lines are found at most ancient monuments and sacred places. Monuments serve to reveal or mark this network by connecting them together. The word 'Ley' is akin to leoht (light illumination) and the middle English word 'lea' meaning 'pasture land,' a meadow that is open to the sun and therefore, at times, drenched with light.

A single vortex is described as a region of fluid where the flow is mostly a spinning motion about an imaginary axis, straight or curved. That motion pattern is called a vortical flow and you can imagine it as a whirlpool similar to that in the wake of boat, or the winds surrounding hurricanes, tornadoes and dust devils. Once formed, vortices can move, stretch, twist, and interact in complex ways.

So, vortices appear to be points of power or energy, which have the capacity to move, stretch, twist, and interact in complex ways on the earth, and ley lines are the relationships between these energy points.

To explain in a simpler form, if you can imagine the analogy of vortices as being acupressure points on your body then the ley lines between them are meridians on the skin. The meridian system is also called a channel network, and in traditional Chinese medicine is the belief about a path through which life-energy known as 'qi' flows.

The study of the science of consciousness began in the mid-1800s, when a group of German philosophers began to ask whether or not consciousness could be studied scientifically. Today, the journal of consciousness studies contains a wide variety of reflections by academic scholars and researchers in anatomy, computation, physiology, psychology, artificial intelligence, religion, philosophy, and more.

Many of those who study the science of consciousness believe that as the earth goes through this next transition, the structure of our planet will change and a transformation of consciousness will arise. It is through the changing of all universal energies that the earth takes its rightful place, keeping in harmony with all other cosmic phenomena in the galaxy and universe.

With this change, we are likely to see new scientific discoveries and new medical awareness in energy consciousness that we cannot see but will knowingly be there. We are drawn towards this shift at the essence of our very being.

I feel we are all greatly privileged to be living in this moment when new energy formations and a shift of consciousness is so evidently happening to give us greater meaning and understanding. As a heart-centred entrepreneur, it is through your contribution that you will feel a reconnection with the energy of life and be at one with our amazing world.

Note: If want to read further on the Science of Consciousness visit: www.mindscience.org. There is also the Mind Project at www.mind.ilstu.edu.

There are articles related to many aspects of what is covered in this chapter at www.energy-shifter.com. I can also recommend the science fiction book The Corridors Of Time by Poul Anderson. Although published in 1966 it is a great read with an interesting perspective on time travel.

You must take
personal responsibility.
You cannot change
the circumstances,
the seasons,
or the wind,
but you can
change yourself.
That is something
you have charge of.

Jim Rohn

Chapter Eighteen

Creating the Space Where Miracles Happen
The One-Degree Shift to Change Your Destiny

Something I've learned in the course of my work is that it doesn't matter how much money, time, and effort you throw into something; if it's off course, if it's not part of your soul journey, it won't work.

Knowing you're off course when it isn't working out as planned gives you the opportunity to do something about it. Admitting there's a problem can be difficult, especially if you stand to lose face with family and friends.

Being stubborn reminds me of what is reputed to be Canada's favourite joke. It goes like this: An American battleship is lost at sea in thick fog. The first mate excitedly reports a light ahead, so the captain immediately radios the vessel, demanding it divert its course to avoid collision. A Canadian voice responds to the captain, recommending the battleship changes its own course.

The US captain is outraged. 'This is the captain of a US Navy ship, I say again, divert your course'.

'No', says the Canadian calmly. The US captain is beside himself. 'This is the USS Lincoln', he explodes, 'I demand that YOU change your course'.

There are a few moments' pause before the Canadian replies, 'This is a lighthouse, sir. Your call.'

I imagine this joke has put a smile on your face. If you're like me, I'm sure at times you've been too stubborn or have had your head stuck firmly in the sand, to the detriment of being able to move forward. It happens to the best of us at some point.

Sometimes, a simple shift is all it takes to get out of the rut. There's a process I'd like to share with you. It began over 37 years ago when the great late philosopher and author Sydney Banks discovered three principles to explain how humans create their own experience of life.

His discovery led to remarkable transformations amongst people from all walks of life. Sydney Banks, a true visionary, knew that when people learned of the powerful resources that lie within, miracles would occur and their lives would change forever more.

The three principles of divine mind, consciousness, and thought enable individuals to experience powerful insights and beautiful changes in their lives. Psychologists, therapists, teachers, police officers and thousands of other people, including many in jails, prisons, and drug rehabilitation facilities have turned their lives around, finding hope, happiness, and success using these principles.

Here are Sydney Bank's three principles, having the capacity to change people's lives:

1. The Principle of Mind.

There is an ever-present energy and intelligence behind life. We accept that it exists, such as the sun rising in the morning, rivers flowing to the sea, saplings becoming trees; life is life. It is not in control and has no inherent morality or viewpoint.

2. The Principle of Consciousness.

As human beings, we all have the capacity to be aware and experience life. The level of our awareness determines the quality of that experience. It is a universal phenomenon.

3. The Principle of Thought.

Thought is the vehicle we create our individual experience from. Thought is the link between the formless world of pure potentiality and the created world of form.

Sydney Banks differentiated between the ego mind (small mind) and the divine mind (big mind) as being the universal mind, the intelligence of literally all things in this world and any other world. He explained that this is the mind you should be looking for, because it has the power to guide you through life. This is the principle of mind.

The principle of consciousness is the higher-powered energy recognised in many fields, from scientists and mystics to religious groups and even atheists. Put simply, it's an acknowledgment that there is something far bigger than our personal view. The more connected you are with that part of yourself, the more beautiful your life will be.

Consciousness, according to Sydney, gives us the ability to realise the existence of life. He said that consciousness is infinite. It has a number of levels and there is no end to it. It means there is no end to you finding beauty, love, and understanding in this world.

Sydney Bank's principles reminded me of the story behind the 2003 comedy Bruce Almighty, starring Jim Carrey. Bruce, being down on his luck, complains to God that he isn't doing his job properly. God meets with Bruce in an empty warehouse where he gives Bruce the opportunity of being God for a week. Initially, Bruce is elated and uses his powers for all sorts of personal gains and in seeking revenge on those he perceives as having wronged him.

As the film progresses, Bruce starts to hear voices in his head; he can't understand why. Later, he encounters God on Mount Everest, where he explains the voices are prayers, which Bruce, acting as God, must deal with.

To begin with God met Bruce at ground level in the warehouse and then on top of Mount Everest, overlooking the world; the perception being that pure consciousness is a formless potential, and we all experience it at different levels. When our level changes, our view changes. The higher up we experience consciousness, the clearer our view.

In the film, Bruce of course creates all sort of chaos before he finally sorts his life out, becoming a humbler, nicer, happier person, with greater clarity and experiencing the world from a higher level of consciousness and awareness. He is then able to respond to whatever is happening around him more insightfully. The world in turn reacts positively. This goes someway to explaining the principle of consciousness, when applied to our lives positively.

The third piece of Sydney Bank's three principles is the creative principle: thought.

Sydney said, "You're only one thought away from happiness, you're only one thought away from sadness. The secret is thought. It's the missing link that everybody in the world is looking for.

> "Mind is the intelligence of all things. Consciousness makes you aware; and thought is like the rudder of a ship. It guides you through life. If you learn to use the rudder properly, you can guide your way through life far better than you ever imagined."

According to Jamie Smart, an internationally renowned writer, speaker, coach, and consultant, the only thing that keeps a person 'stuck in a rut' is superstitious thinking, the mistaken belief in feeling something other than thought in the moment. As soon as you realise you're feeling your thinking, it's a sign that the system is self-correcting and you're aligned with how life really works.

Lucy, a coaching client of mine was always in a race to get things done, describing herself as being in manic mode; "There's always so much to catch up on."

Lucy's frustration lies in her feelings of not building her business quickly enough. Work and checklists her daily focus. This particular session, I immediately sensed Lucy was stressed out, her conversation was rapid and darting from explaining one completed task to the next one which was on her list still to do.

"Stop! Take a breather" I exclaimed. Sharing my feelings with Lucy, I began by asking why she felt she had to work so hard. As we talked, she became very emotional.

Eventually, she spoke about her upbringing, how she still felt she was a disappointment to her parents' high expectations of her. If she wasn't working hard enough she felt she was letting her parents down. She also felt anyone needing time off or being too sick to work was being lazy. By keeping herself constantly busy and task oriented, she was putting herself under immense pressure and her health at risk too.

Our conversation continued, exploring Lucy's thinking patterns and associated feelings, until we reached a few moments of reflective silence.

Lucy's breakthrough response came in a stronger, more empowered voice. In those few moments Lucy realised that any thoughts she had of having to work hard were entirely her own. In doing so, she has the power to change her thoughts, replacing them with new, more supportive thoughts.

As our session ended, Lucy stated she was feeling lighter, as if a huge burden was lifted from her shoulders. With her consciousness and clarity raised, she was now in a better place to make personal and business decisions and to move forward positively.

A few days later, I received an email from Lucy thanking me from the bottom of her heart. In just a few days Lucy had reconnected to many of the joys of life she'd sidelined in her manic race to be successful. In return, the world was responding with invitations to meet old friends and her partner suggesting a longed-for holiday. I had no doubt that more clients and increased income were on the horizon too with a happier and more relaxed Lucy.

Lucy's story is an example of gaining insight leading to transformation as part of the soul journey. In his book The Insight Revolution, Michael Neill says that this realisation was a game changer because he knew he could have fresh thinking at any moment. He writes the formula for miracles in the form of two psycho-spiritual equations:

$$\text{Mind} + \text{Thought} + \text{Consciousness} = \text{Reality}$$
$$\text{Mind} + \text{New Thought} + \text{Consciousness} = \text{New Reality}$$

Jamie Smart refers to a rise in consciousness as a kind of penicillin for the mind. Penicillin helps heal physical bodies to overcome illness. Similarly, a rise in consciousness can transform or eliminate huge amounts of habitual thinking. Penicillin goes to wherever it's needed in the body, and a rise in consciousness goes to wherever it's needed in the person's psyche. When this happens, well-being occurs while problems diminish or fall away completely.

Pause for a few thoughtful moments.

While on the subject of making a one percent shift in consciousness leading to transformation here's another thought; studies show that approximately four to six percent of the world's population makes more than $100,000, which is a six-figure income or more.

Many others are stuck below the poverty line. Can you imagine how powerful it would be if there was a one-percent shift in the world's consciousness? This would be phenomenal.

A one-degree shift will change your destiny when you create the space for miracles to happen.

> My greatest challenge has been to change the mindset of people. Mindsets play strange tricks on us. We see things the way our minds have instructed our eyes to see.
>
> Muhammad Yunus

Chapter Nineteen

You Were Born a Creative Genius
Intuition, Your Fail-Safe Navigation System

At heart, we're all born creative geniuses in our own way, with an inner knowing, a wisdom, a feeling, a heightened intuition.

If you pay attention to this wisdom, you will develop it over time, fine-tuning it. It will lead you to your ideal home, your ideal job, and your soul mate. It will connect you with your business angels at the very time you need them. It just happens, as if by magic.

Intuition is your built-in fail-safe satellite navigation system throughout your life. Your inner wisdom is tuned to the universal mind, which is why when you listen to intuition it works. It's a short circuit to the outer wisdom of the universe.

Your wisdom can save you time and money, but it can also save you from heartache and tears too.

Nicole, a business colleague of mine, was having pre-wedding jitters. Convinced it was normal to feel this way before her wedding, she brushed off any misgivings with logical thinking. "It's to be expected, I'm sure everyone has pre-wedding nerves. That's all it is."

However, her inner knowing was having none of it, her nights becoming increasingly disturbed with troubled, unsettling dreams. Plans for the wedding began to be disrupted.

Everything from her dress alterations being too tight to receiving a call from the limousine company who'd accidentally double-booked her wedding car and could not give her the limousine she'd originally ordered for the wedding.

The last straw was the catering company going into liquidation and her mother falling ill with a mysterious stomach bug. Nicole postponed the wedding for three months.

During this time, she discovered her fiancé was having an affair with a colleague in his workspace. Suddenly, everything fitted together like a puzzle. She called off the wedding, meeting Mr. Right a few months later. Nicole's intuition knew best and was crying out for her to listen to it and not make the biggest mistake of her life.

Has intuition ever played out in your life in seemingly strange situations that become clear at a later date? The universe always knows what is right for you. All you have to do is pay attention to it.

In business, intuition is often overlooked as something a bit wacky or cuckoo, but that's far from the truth. Donald Trump once declared he'd "built a multi-billion dollar empire using intuition."

I like thinking big. If you're going to be thinking anything, you might as well think big. Donald Trump

Oprah Winfrey, speaking to a group of businesswomen in Chicago, declared,

"My business skills have come from being guided by my inner self, my intuition."

Intuition differs greatly from person to person. Sometimes it's having a 'gut feeling' about what to do next in a difficult situation. At other times, it's a specific emotional trigger indicating a yes or a no answer. Then there is the psychic definition, where information is gleaned about other people, places, or past and future events. Intuition can be a combination of all of these and more.

In Malcolm Gladwell's book Blink, he begins with the story of an ancient Greek statue that came onto the art market. The Getty Museum was interested in purchasing it. The asking price was just under ten million dollars.

All the normal background checks were carried out as to the authenticity of the statue. Experts determined the marble came from the ancient Cape Varthy quarry. It had a thin layer of calcite, a substance that accumulates on statues over hundreds of thousands of years. The investigation took over 14 months before the Getty staff concluded the statue to be genuine. They went ahead with the purchase. Shortly afterwards, Federico Zert, an art historian, was invited to see the statue when it went on display and immediately decided it was a fake.

Another art historian sensed that although the form was correct, the work lacked spirit. A third expert felt a wave of intuitive repulsion when he first laid eyes on the statue.

The Getty staff decided to make further investigations. It was then discovered the statue was a fake. It had been very skillfully sculpted by forgers in Rome. The teams of analysts had been wrong. The historians who relied on intuition were right.

Intuition: it affects your business profits positively.

There is a huge difference in using intuition in business as opposed to relying on physical data. Research conducted by Douglas Dean on the relationship between intuition and business success at the New Jersey Institute of Technology found that over 80 percent of executives whose business profits had more than doubled in the past five years had above pre-cognitive intuitive powers.

Management professor Weston Agor of the University of Texas in El Paso found that of the 2,000 managers he tested, higher-level managers gained top scores in intuition. He discovered while most executives first of all digested all the relevant information and data available, when there was conflicting or incomplete data, they used intuition to reach their conclusion.

Alongside Donald Trump and Oprah Winfrey, Andrew Carnegie, John D. Rockefeller, Conrad Hilton, Alan Sugar, Steve Jobs, and Richard Branson have all claimed to use intuition positively in business.

Intuition is further increased by introducing creativity tools, music, dance, meditation, visualization, and outside-of-the-box activities engaging your big (divine) mind. The success of accelerated learning, often referred to as power training embraces many activities to heighten and stimulate your intuition as part of the learning process.

Your business angels are guided by intuition, they all have fine-tuned this ability. Fine-tuning your intuition and using it wisely gives your life and business the Midas touch.

"Our greatness
lies not so much
in being able
to remake the world
as being able
to remake
ourselves."

Gandhi

Chapter Twenty

Evolving and Taking Your Place In The World
Your Time is Now!

Everything you'll ever need is already there. It really is all inside of you. You don't need to have a story where you've been shot, declared bankrupt, and then made millions - or to have been lost in the outback for six months and survived on water droplets and cactus plants. You have your own unique, authentic story. It is your truth.

Your gifts, talents, and contributions are your most valuable assets and a true legacy for the world. You express your purpose through your business. When you are on the right path for you, you will feel alive. Your business will be alive. Your life will become easier, your business will grow, and you will receive the financial rewards you deserve.

When you are on the right path for you, shining like a bright diamond glittering in the snow, be aware that dark forces or negative people are at times attracted to that bright shiny light too, because opposites attract. Protecting yourself, being aware and having the right business angels by your side will prevent this from becoming a problem.

This book has shared with you the secrets to the sacred path of the business angels and the universal knowledge and power available to you. If you work through all seven steps of the business angel plan and seek out the seven key people to help you along the way – they will appear just when you need them.

As your guide, my intention is to get you on to the sacred path of the business angels to enable you to take your place in the world alongside the great masters, where you can add your contribution to the universal database. In doing so, your work will be an expression of who you are, and who you were always meant to be.

To help guide you from your initial idea, spark it into a unique, creative, and inspirational action plan just for you and your business, join me online at:

www.7businessangels.com to
download your 7-Step Business Angel Plan Template
entering access code:
BAGifts for your download.

You will also be able to download your free copy of an incredibly inspirational and motivational PDF e-book 'Business Angel Wisdom & Insights' with tips, business knowledge and favourite quotes and also where you can connect with business angels worldwide on the sacred path of successful entrepreneurs.

I do hope you've enjoyed our journey together and that you've have had some fun along the way too. Do join me online and I'd love you to share your thoughts and any testimonials with me too.

"When you reach for the stars, you are reaching for the farthest thing out there. When you reach deep inside yourself, it is the same thing, but in the opposite direction. If you reach in both directions, you will have spanned the universe."

- Vera Nazarian, The Perpetual Calendar of Inspiration

Resources

Dr Lisa Turner – The Spiritual Scientist - www.psycademy.com

Kimberley Lovell - Spiritual Intuitive Theta Healer & Holistic Business Mentor - www.KimberleyLovell.com & www.SacredMoneyArchetypes.com

Norma Reid - www.fromdreamstoreality.ca

Jim J. Doyle - Business healer, communications coach, keynote speaker - www.jimjdoyle.com

Dorina Lanza – Wealth Strategies – http://dorinalanza.com

Lynne McTaggart - The Intention Experiment
http://theintentionexperiment.com

The Worlds First 3-D Human AurImaging Technology
http://wwwsedonacreativelife.com/pre0840.html
http://krishnamadappa.com
Gas Discharge Visualisation (GDV) Device
http://www.youtube.com/watch?v=DhBYqkos-Xk
http://korotkov.org

Konstantin Korotkov capturing the timing of disembodiment http://consciouslifenews.com/scientist-photographs-soul-leaving-body/#

http://topdocumentaryfilms.com/water-great-mystery
https://www.deepakchopra.com
http://www.bentleymotors.com/distinguished_heritage/history

George Gurdijeff - www.mindscience.org

www.mind.ilstu.edu

www.energy-shifter.com

Books

The Naked Brain, Richard Restak

A Brief History of Time, Stephen Hawking

The Inside Out Revolution, Michael Neil

Our True Identity, Three Principles, Elsie Spittle

The Enlightened Gardener, Sydney Banks

Second Chance, Syd Banks

Clarity, Clear Mind, Better Performance, Bigger Results, Jamie Smart

The Insight Revolution, Michael Neill

Blink, Malcolm Gladwell

Emotion, Dr. Candace Pert, Phd

Holistic Business Destiny Reading

Do you want to find the creative business path destiny always had in mind for you?

And finally stop running round in circles searching for solutions and instead get to the heart of the real issues preventing you from reaching your true potential?

By having a 'one to one' 60 Minute Holistic Business Destiny Reading, I will help you to:

- Find the right direction for you … and finally discover the true potential that lies in your business …
- Turn your ideas into creative solutions to generate the income you want … and without being a slave to your business …
- Hone in on issues and problems which are likely to blight your path to success … and provide solutions
- Identify the money centre of your business … and how to access the hidden money that's already there (but you can't see it).

Book online here:
www.spiritofvenus.co.uk/businessdestinyreading

As a heart-centred entrepreneur, you are meant to shine. You are meant to share your gifts and talents with the world. People are waiting for your solution. It is your duty to meet this need. It's time to stop searching … and finally get it right.

www.ingramcontent.com/pod-product-compliance
Lightning Source LLC
Chambersburg PA
CBHW051056160426
43193CB00010B/1200